J. H Reeves

The Orange County Stud Book

J. H Reeves

The Orange County Stud Book

ISBN/EAN: 9783744678766

Printed in Europe, USA, Canada, Australia, Japan

Cover: Foto ©ninafisch / pixelio.de

More available books at **www.hansebooks.com**

ORANGE COUNTY STUD BOOK,

GIVING A HISTORY OF

ALL NOTED STALLIONS

BRED AND RAISED IN ORANGE COUNTY;

TOGETHER WITH

SYMPTOMS AND TREATMENT OF THE DISEASES OF THE HORSE,

BY

J. H. REEVES, V. S.

PUBLISHED BY

DAVIDSON & CO.,
86 Nassau St., New York
1875.

INTRODUCTION.

THE author of this little work, a native, and for years a resident of Orange County, and one whose avocation has thrown him much into the society of her horsemen, and consequently enabled him to acquire much valuable information in regard to the breeding of horses in that county, and the history and pedigree of its celebrated animals, in presenting his book to the public, hopes that, in estimating its value, the reliability, novelty, and usefulness of its statements, rather than the number of its pages, will be taken into consideration by the reader. It is probable that no useful animal is more affected by climate and food than the horse; and while the climate of the County of Orange seems favorable to the production of the horse, and its rich pastures and fine meadows afford the elements for developing the finest forms and most enduring constitutions, it is only by a judicious system of breeding that to these two requisites of a *good* horse, the third, that of speed, can be added.

Our ideas of the system of breeding which should be adopted in order to be successful, and the reasons upon which they are founded, constitute our first article. It contains no idle dogmas or worthless and fantastic theories, calculated to lead the earnest and honest searcher for useful knowledge into gross errors and mistakes, but rather a collection of rules, precepts, and facts, deduced from long experience in and close observation of all matters pertaining to the subject.

While it is an undeniable fact that many fast trotters have been bred and raised by persons who had no knowledge of these principles, yet if the pedigree of such could be correctly traced, it would be found that the breeders thereof have almost invariably conformed unintentionally to these established rules, and that, consequently, instead of the progeny being simply the result of chance, it was produced under and in strict accordance with the fixed rule of the law of nature — that "like will produce like."

In proof of the soundness of our theory in regard to breeding, we shall follow the above-mentioned article with the pedigree and history of a few of the most celebrated stock horses which have been produced in Orange County, which, if carefully perused, cannot fail to convince the reader of the infallibility of the law of reproduction. And while our work is designed more particularly for those who, in consequence of their interest therein, may properly be styled "horsemen," yet we trust that it will not be altogether without interest to the general reader, and that he may obtain some useful information in regard to the animal which contributes so much to the comfort and pleasure of mankind, and which represents so largely the wealth of our citizens.

The author has spent much time in obtaining the reliable pedigree and history of the noted stallion,

American Star; and facts are herein disclosed in regard to the history of Rysdyk's Hambletonian never before made public. As these are now universally regarded as the representative stock horses of Orange County, and as the history of each is replete with interest, much more might have been written; having concluded, however, to offer our book at a price within the reach of all, we have been compelled to condense it in this as well as in many other particulars. We have also appended a brief treatise on the diseases of horses and the treatment thereof, which will be found to be worth the price of the book ten-fold to every horse owner.

BREEDING

IN ORANGE COUNTY.

Having briefly referred to the general subject of breeding horses in the foregoing article, we pass to notice the history and results thereof in Orange County, in which county the subject has received great attention, and has been rendered exceedingly profitable to those who have engaged judiciously therein. Indeed, from the time when the attention of the citizens of this county was first drawn to this subject, the standard of trotting horses throughout the country has been gradually elevated, and their speed so increased, that with the present established record of 2.17, it would seem that it has now reached its lowest second, and that not much greater achievements could reasonably be expected from horseflesh.

While the breeding of running horses has been in vogue for years, and *their* contests upon the turf is a time-honored and ancient amusement, the first stallion that we ever saw advertised as possessing trotting qualities was Imported Bellfounder, in the year 1832. He was a bright bay, with black main, tail, and legs, standing fifteen hands high; and his superior blood, symmetry of form, and action, excelled all other stallions. He was allowed, by the best judges in Norfolk, England, to be the fastest and best-bred stallion ever sent out of that country. No doubt he was, for, as a proof, he stayed here only one year, and was then taken back. Bellfounder made the season at Washingtonville, with full pedigree given, at twenty-five dollars to insure a mare in foal. And here, well may we mention, that forty years ago, twenty-five dollars made the farmers of Orange County open their eyes, for at that time, it is a fact well known, that the *price* of service was looked at, *not* pedigree.

Bellfounder at that time was said to have trotted seventeen miles in an hour. Notwithstanding what was then considered an exorbitant price, Bellfounder was patronised, for the Crabtree mare was his daughter, and the mother of J. D. Sayer's Harry Clay, who has proved himself a trotter, and the sire of trotters. Bellfounder was the sire of the Charles Kent mare, the mother of the celebrated stallion Hambletonian, the property of the late Wm. M. Rysdyk, of Chester, Orange County, N. Y. Of this horse and his get, a place will be found in this book. We pass through the years of our Hylanders, Hickories, Wild Airs, Liberties, Lances, Bolivars, Ottoways, Bullfrogs, and a host of others, many of whose get made good mothers, properly bred, for they were all bred up. (See article on breeding.) There was not much change in breeding valuable horses until about the spring of 1847, when Abdallah came into this county. He was a big, coarse, homely horse; and then the farmers first began to look at and turn their attention, many of them, to *pedigree* and *blood*. This horse Abdallah was almost if not *the* first point made in Orange County in bringing the breeding of trotters to the standard it has at the present time. Black Hawk came into the county next, and left some good colts. His mare colts have made some of our best breeders. Charles Bull, of the town of Blooming Grove has a mare sired by Black Hawk that has raised him six colts by Hambletonian, all horse colts, and have been sold young. He has one foaled in 1871. And these colts have averaged Mr. Bull two thousand four hundred dollars. Other mares by Black Hawk are valued highly as breeders. Black Hawk died in Montgomery, July, 1853.

Cassius M. Clay, Jr., made his appearance here in the spring of 1852. His get has been of great value for breeding purposes, as it gave us more *size*, more *bone*, and *speed*. He left a large number of good ones in this county. His price for service was twenty dollars, which was thought to be extravagant by those who patronised him. J. D. Sayer's Harry Clay was one of his get—was foaled in the spring of 1853,—was kept for service in this county until he was sold in 1862 to Harry Dater, of New York, for five thousand dollars. This horse was a stock horse that improved our breeds for *bone, size,* and *speed.* Of his get many are of note on the turf, his mares are highly appreciated on our breeding farms, and his horse colts kept as stallions have been sold at *high figures* and left our county. One is still here kept for service; this is Black Harry Clay, foaled in the spring of 1859. He was bred by Wm. Owen, and owned by him and Brad. P. Doty, but has always been under the control of Brad. This horse is a trotter, and his get are trotters. One of his colts was sold to Gen. Kilpatrick for four thousand dollars in gold, and taken to Chili. Cassius M. Clay, the sire of Cassius M. Clay, Jr., stood for service in Montgomery, and died in the same stable that the Black Hawk died in, July, 1854. He was *driven* to death, and Black Hawk *doctored* to death. As this family of horses all have their representatives at the present day, we must give space and time for those that are still on the stage of action. We will leave this by giving a history of the celebrated stallion Hambletonian and his get.

HISTORY

OF THE

HORSE HAMBLETONIAN,

The Property of the late Wm. M. Rysdyk.

The pedigree of this celebrated horse is familiar to almost every horseman throughout the civilized world; indeed, perhaps no single horse ever foaled has won from his own intrinsic merits such an extensive and enduring reputation.

He was by Abdallah, the grandson of the renowned imported Messenger; his dam the Charles Kent mare, and she by imported Bellfounder.

Abdallah was kept for mares at Chester, Orange County, in the years eighteen hundred and forty-seven and eight, at twenty dollars to insure a colt. In the latter year, Jonas Seely, of the same town, owned this Charles Kent mare, and bred her to the horse Abdallah. She proved with foal, and on the fifteenth day of May, eighteen hundred and forty-nine, gave birth to the colt which since has become so famous throughout the land under the name of Hambletonian.

The mare, with her colt by her side, was sold by Mr. Seely to the late William M. Rysdyk, for the sum of one hundred and twenty-five dollars. The circumstances of Mr. Rysdyk were at this time very limited, and it was only through the assistance of friends that he was enabled to effect the purchase even at the low figures named by the owner. From the price paid we may readily infer that there was nothing very attractive or extraordinary either in the appearance of the dam or her foal. The colt, however, under the careful management of his new owner, rapidly improved, and was shown the same fall at the fair of the Orange County Agricultural Society at Goshen.

At this exhibition he was led by the side of a horse, and was equipped with a white bridle, martingals, and girth, a fact often spoken of by men who were boys at that time. This brought the colt into some little notoriety, which arose, perhaps, more from the style of his equipment than anything else, as it was something novel in those days to see one so young exhibited in that style and manner. This was in the fall of eighteen hundred and forty-nine, and he was again shown in the fall of eighteen hundred and fifty, at the same place and under circumstances equally as well calculated to attract attention.

In the spring of eighteen hundred and fifty-one, we saw him again, at the residence of his owner, and so greatly had he improved, and so rapid had been his growth, that, although he was but two years old, he resembled in almost every particular a fully-developed horse.

Mr. Rysdyk, during this season, allowed him to cover four mares, as appears by Mr. R's. books, which we have been kindly permitted to inspect, and to which we are indebted for much of the information hereinafter contained.

He got three colts from these mares (two horses and one mare), and no price is charged for the services upon the book, an omission, however, which never thereafter occurs. One of these colts soon thereafter came into the hands of Major J. Seeley Edsall, of Goshen, and under his careful handling soon proved himself a superior horse.

The Major kept him for mares four years at Goshen, and then sold him to Mr. Alexander, of Kentucky; he however, had in the meantime become the father of the filly now so widely known throughout this country as Goldsmith's Maid. We might mention many other "good ones" from him, but for the present must trace the history of his sire.

In speaking of this—Hambletonian's first season—it is a fact worthy of remark, that a very large percentage of his progeny thus far in his prolific career have been males, and that while large numbers of *them* have from time to time covered themselves with glory in their contests upon the turf, the reputation of the old horse as a father of trotters would scarcely arise above mediocrity were it entirely dependant upon the exploits of his daughters.

In the spring of eighteen hundred and fifty-two he was offered for service to a limited number of mares at twenty-five dollars to insure a colt. While we cannot assert that the practice of limiting the number of mares to be served during the season was inaugurated by Mr. Rysdyk at this time, yet it is a fact which cannot be gainsayed, that his example has been rigidly followed ever since by the owners of stallions in their advertisements at least. During this season he served seventeen mares and got thirteen colts. In the fall he was taken to the Island to be trained as a trotter, and after going through a term of three months of this kind of education, he returned to Chester, without having made any public record of his performance upon the turf. Notwithstanding the assertion of the renowned Hiram Woodruff, that the Abdallahs could endure more early training than almost any other breed of horses, we are credibly informed that this son of Abdallah was retired from the turf thus early in consequence of his inability to withstand its severe exactions.

In the spring of eighteen hundred and fifty-three he was advertised for service. His full pedigree was given, and twenty-five dollars was again asked to insure a colt.

The breeders of Orange County, at this early day in the history of the horse, began to appreciate his fine qualities, and to extend to him a liberal patronage, as he covered during this season one hundred and one mares, and got seventy-eight colts. His success as a stock horse was now fully assured, and without any brilliant performance upon the turf, or any of that puffing and blowing so frequently used both to create and perpetuate the reputation of stallions, he entered upon a career never equaled in the annals of horse-breeding. In the spring of eighteen hundred and fifty-four a similar advertisement appeared, with the single exception that the price was raised to thirty-five dollars. Eighty-eight mares were served, and sixty-three colts were paid for. In eighteen hundred and fifty-five, at the same place and price, he served eighty-nine mares, and sixty-four colts were paid for

B

In eighteen hundred and fifty-six, eighty-seven mares and sixty-four colts. In eighteen hundred and fifty-seven, eighty-seven mares and sixty-three colts. In eighteen hundred and fifty-eight, seventy-two mares and fifty-four colts. In eighteen hundred and fifty-nine, ninety-five mares and sixty-six colts. In eighteen hundred and sixty, one hundred and six mares and seventy-two colts. In eighteen hundred and sixty-one, ninety-eight mares and sixty-eight colts. In eighteen hundred and sixty-two, one hundred and fifty-eight mares and one hundred and eleven colts were paid for. During these preceding nine years he stood a part of the time at Goshen, but principally at his owner's stable in Chester, at thirty-five dollars to insure.

The brilliant performances of his colts upon the turf had now given their sire a national reputation. They were in great demand, and commanded high, and in many instances, exorbitant prices; and the breeding of trotters received a new and greater impetus than ever before throughout the county. A new road to fortune and wealth was opened, and many a farmer, into whose brain the idea of making a dollar in any other way than by the production of milk and butter had never entered, prompted by the success of a neighbor, turned his attention to breeding horses, and forthwith concluded "to put the old mare."

Mr. Rysdyk, taking advantage of this state of affairs, raised his price for the services of Hambletonian to seventy-five dollars, at which price, in the season of eighteen hundred and sixty-three, he covered one hundred and fifty mares, and got ninety-two colts. The next season, eighteen hundred and sixty-four, the price was again raised to one hundred dollars. Two hundred and seventeen mares were covered, and one hundred and forty-eight colts got. In eighteen hundred and sixty-five the price was raised to three hundred dollars to insure, one hundred dollars of which was to be paid at the time of service. During this season one hundred and ninety-three mares were served, and one hundred and twenty-eight colts got. The following season, eighteen hundred and sixty-six, at five hundred dollars, one hundred of which was required to be paid down, he served one hundred and five mares, and got seventy-five colts. In eighteen hundred and sixty-seven, he served seventy-seven mares and got forty-one colts.

As might reasonably have been expected, from the polygamous course of life to which the old horse had for years been subjected, his physical powers became weakened, and during the year eighteen hundred and sixty-eight he was retired from the stud, and covered no mares. Notwithstanding, however, the prognostications of many that he was "played out," a season's rest had a highly beneficial effect upon him, and during the following season he served twenty-one mares and got fourteen colts. In eighteen hundred and seventy he served twenty-two mares and got thirteen colts. In eighteen hundred and seventy-one he was limited to thirty mares, which he served, and from which he got twenty colts, having left some seventy applicants unserved in consequence of this limitation. We have been informed by Mr. Geo. Andrews, under whose management and direction Hambletonian now is, that for the coming season of eighteen hundred and seventy two over one hundred applications have been received, from which number, however, but thirty will be accepted. Upon a recent visit to Chester, the old horse was shown to us by his very gentlemanly manager. Although exhibiting many of the indications of old age, as a matter of course, yet his eye appeared bright and undimmed by years, while his coat was glossy; and those peculiar points which long since have led him to be pronounced the "King of Horses," still stand out in bold relief. While standing in his majestic presence, and remembering the fact that he was the sire of twelve hundred and fifty standing colts, that they or their progeny were represented in almost every state and county throughout the United States, and in almost every country in the civilized world, and that upon their successful contests upon the turf, fortunes had been won again and again, we could not but respect and venerate him. Although, in the natural course of events, the days of the old horse will soon be numbered, yet, upon the undeniable maxim that "like begets like," we shall continue to produce trotters in Orange County for years to come which will maintain our proud and pre-eminent position upon the turf.

The sons and grandsons of the princely old horse are yearly begetting colts superior to themselves, and with our present knowledge of breeding judiciously applied, we have no hesitation in asserting that the speed of trotting horses will still be vastly increased, and that the future Kings and Queens of the turf will hail from Orange County.

THE SONS

OF

OLD HAMBLETONIAN.

In view of the length of time in which Hambletonian has been at the stud, and of the vast number of colts of which, during that time, he has become the sire—as portrayed by the preceding article—it cannot be expected that we will give more than a passing notice of a few of the many celebrated stallions which have sprung from his loins; and the first we will mention is—

Alexander's Hambletonian.

This horse—or as he is more familiarly known in Orange County—Edsall's Hambletonian, was, as we have previously remarked, one of Hambletonian's first get, having been foaled in the year eighteen hundred and fifty-two, out of a mare by Bay Roman, he by Mambrino, and he by Messenger.

He was purchased, when quite young, by Major Edsall, of Goshen, and was kept by him until eighteen hundred and fifty-nine, when he was sold to Mr. Alexander, of Lexington, Kentucky. During the time he was owned by Major Edsall, he proved himself not only to be very speedy, but also one of the finest stock horses ever produced. It is said that, during the war, he was stolen by the rebels, and that Alexander offered a reward of one thousand dollars for his recovery. Stimulated by this liberal reward, parties immediately set out for his recapture, and one of the pursuants, mounted upon a thorough-bred mare, succeeded in overtaking the thief, when a conflict with arms commenced, during which the stallion was unfortunately accidentally shot. He was returned to his owner, and the reward paid; but, either from the effects of the wound, or from over-exertion, he died very soon thereafter. He was the sire of Goldsmith's Maid, now the acknowledged Queen of the

Turf; of Major Edsall, a very fast stallion; and of many other good ones not so well known; indeed, it is almost the universal opinion of the experienced horsemen of the county, that had he remained therein he would long ere this have acquired a reputation as a stock horse not even second to his sire.

Edward Everett,

(Formerly Major Winfield), has recently, in consequence of the achievements of his colts, greatly distinguished himself as a stock horse. His dam is said to have been by imported Margrave, and was formerly owned and used under the saddle by the Hon. Thomas George, of this county. He bred her to Hambletonian; and, although recognizing the superior qualities of his mare, yet, for some reason, he gave the colt to Sheriff Lillum, upon condition that he would keep the mare until the colt was weaned. In connection with this fact, it may be mentioned, that Judge George bought one of Everett's sons, which has since become noted, viz., Mountain Boy, when four years old; but as this horse at that time showed nothing very promising, to say the least, he sold him to Esquire Bingham, soon after, for one hundred and fifty dollars.

Everett is also the sire of Judge Fullerton and Joe Elliott, who are of themselves enough to demonstrate the great value of their sire. He was purchased by Robert Bonner, for twenty thousand dollars, and is now standing at the Lagrange Farm, in this county, under the management of Mr. Wm. H. Keetch.

Volunteer.

While the success of a stallion, either as a trotter or as a stock producer, must depend very much upon his own intrinsic merits, yet, in both of these particulars, much also depends upon his management and the care and treatment which he receives at the hands or by the direction of his owner. In this particular, Volunteer has been extremely fortunate. His owner,

Mr. Alden Goldsmith, is one of the most intelligent and practical breeders in the county, and, indeed, may justly be considered the pioneer breeder of trotters therein. His great experience and sound judgment has led him to adopt a judicious system of crossing this horse with mares of his own, the results of which have of themselves established a reputation for the horse which is exceedingly enviable. His dam was by Young Patriot, a descendant of Messenger; and his colts are generally very good sized, strong and handsome.

Among the speedy ones, we may mention Hamlet, W. H. Allen, Huntress, and Bodine; while we understand that a Whirlwind will soon appear upon the turf which will astonish the world.

Middletown.

Recent exploits of the colts of this horse have greatly increased his popularity as a breeder, and have placed him in the foremost rank of stallions, some horsemen even predicting that he is the "coming stock horse." He is out of a mare by American Eclipse, a grandson of Messenger, and thus has a combination of the very best strains of the Messenger blood.

Although his colts are quite young, yet one of them —Music, owned by that expert horseman and judicious trainer, William Trimble, of Newburgh—a four-year-old, out of a second Star mare, has shown herself to be extremely fast upon several occasions.

Middletown has been absent from the county for several months, but we are glad to learn that he will make the coming season at Middletown, and we doubt not but that many of our breeders will avail themselves of his services.

Happy Medium.

The mother of this stallion was the renowned Princess, that so frequently and so gamely disputed the supremacy of the turf with Flora Temple, which is probably all the encomium he needs at our hands.

He was sold last season by Mr. Fowler Galloway, to parties in Philadelphia, for a large price; yet the investment will undoubtedly be exceedingly profitable to his present owners, as we understood he afterwards covered one hundred mares at one hundred and fifty dollars for the season. Mr. J. S. Edsall, who has been the fortunate owner of some of the very best stock ever produced in the county, has a very fine bay stallion by him, out of a Black Hawk mare.

Idol.

Mr. Backman, the owner of this fine young horse, is the most extensive breeder of trotters in the world. And inasmuch as, since the establishment of his large business at Stonyford, he has almost monopolized the services of Old Hambletonian and consequently has become the owner of a large number of his colts, it will not be within the scope of our little volume to give a detailed description of the many which are worthy thereof. We have selected Idol, not only as our favorite, but as the recognized head of his stud, to fill the small space we have to spare. He is one of the best proportioned animals in the county—handsome, intelligent, with fine limbs and gait. He is out of a mare by Harry Clay; second dam *said* to be by Terror. Although Mr. Backman may have evidence sufficient to prove the latter fact, yet, notwithstanding, we have known this grandam for years, and always believed, from her appearance, that she was well bred; it was never discovered that she had the pedigree now claimed for her, until after she became the property of Mr. Backman. The dam of Idol was bred by Lewis Tuthill, of Unionville, and was sold by him when she was three years old for one hundred dollars.

Since that time, colts have been raised from her of sufficient value to amount to one or two very fine fortunes. The objection will undoubtedly be raised by some that Idol has Clay blood in his veins, and that his value is thereby considerably decreased. Permit us, however, to remark just here, that, while we are willing to acknowledge that the Clays as trotters have not proved a success, we nevertheless consider the mares of this breed of great value as breeders. They are natural trotters, with splendid action and lots of speed, but have generally developed a "soft spot,"—in other words, are deficient in staying qualities. This single defect, we have no doubt, will be remedied by judicious crossing; and we confidently predict, that the time is not far distant, when these mares will be almost, if not quite, as highly prized for breeders as the Stars.

Idol's colts are very promising; and we feel confident that, as soon as they acquire sufficient age, will duly honor their parentage.

Sayer's Guy Miller.

This horse was bred by Mr. Richard Sears, of Orange County (now deceased), who lived on a large farm some three miles south from the Village of Goshen, and had given much time and attention to the breeding of fine horses, and would undoubtedly have realized his highest anticipations could he have lived to see the progeny of Guy Miller in its present stage of development. Sayer's Guy Miller was foaled in the spring of eighteen hundred and sixty-three, and was purchased by Mr. Daniel Sayer, of Unionville, Orange County, N. Y., at the public sale of Mr. Sears' estate, in the spring of eighteen hundred and sixty-five, for the sum of eleven hundred and fifty dollars. This horse was sired by Galloway's Guy Miller, and he by Hambletonian. The dam of Sayer's Guy Miller was Sharpless Abdallah, by Old Abdallah; grandam, by One-Eyed Hunter, the sire of Flora Temple: inheriting the Messenger blood from both sire and dam. He took the first premium, awarded to colts of his class, for trotting, in Orange County, at the successive ages of three, four, and five years: he also took the first premium at the Agricultural Fair, when competing with some half-dozen of the first of Hambletonian's colts, as being the best stallion in Orange County. Mr. Sayer has bred his horse to a fine Harry Clay mare of his with remarkable success. He sold her first colt, "Tom Sayers," a three-year-old, in the fall of eighteen hundred and seventy, to Budd Doble, for two thousand five hundred dollars, at the time of his winning the three-year-old stake at Middletown, in 2 m. and 56 s., being the same time made by his sire, at the same age. A like sum has been offered for her second colt, and refused. This horse has served mares only at his owner's stable, and at the moderate price of fifty dollars to insure. He served, during the season of eighteen hundred and seventy-one, one hundred and fourteen mares, proving himself a sure foal getter, as well as a source of great profit to his owner.

More fortunately in the horse than in human kind a noble sire more certainly transmits his estimable qualities to his posterity; and while the human kind may bask in the sunshine of ancestral glory, enjoy a secondary fame by keeping himself obscured in the paternal shadow, or claim for himself the undeserved merits of a family name, and with diplomatic skill and through artful devices bear off the laurels belonging to others; the horse kind, before his claims to celebrity and fame are considered, must produce the double
c

assurance of, first, his family record, and secondly, his ability to perform or surpass what his ancestors have done before him. Without ascribing to ourselves the power to unveil the future, even to the extent of one day's fair or foul weather, yet, with a knowledge of facts before us concerning this same Guy Miller, his noble and enduring qualities and many points of excellence, we predict for him, as a getter of trotters, a position second to none among horses, in this country.

AMERICAN STAR

Was a sorrel horse, with star and snip in forehead, two white feet behind, above the pasterns, and about fifteen hands high.

PEDIGREE.

American Star was sired by American Star, he by Cock of the Rock, he by Durock, and he by Romp; Romp by imported Messenger. His dam was by the raceborse, Henry; grandam by Messenger.

That his dam and grandam were both thoroughbreds there is no doubt. His pedigree we shall try to prove, together with his history. For the last five years, the pedigree of the celebrated horse, American Star, has been a subject of much controversy, so much so, that we have taken much time and trouble to furnish a correct history of him. The great value attaching to the progeny of this horse, in the first and second generations, makes it of the utmost importance that breeders should have exact and reliable information as to the blood he possessed. Fortunately, in our travels through Orange, Ulster, and Columbia Counties, in New York, and through a greater part of New Jersey; we think we shall be able, clearly and unmistakably, to give a correct and reliable pedigree and history of the horse, American Star; and supply every link in the chain from the day he was foaled, the property of Henry II. Berry, Esq., of Pompton Plains, Morris County, New Jersey, in June, eighteen hundred and thirty-seven, until he died, the property of Theodore Dusenberry, of Goshen, in February, eighteen hundred and sixty-one. Henry H. Berry sought this horse while owned by Edmond Seeley and Hiram Smith, and recognized him at once as the same horse owned and raised by him till he was seven years of age. This Mr. Berry told us; which, we claim, connects the last link with the first; and we simply mention this because Uncle Edmond did not give him the same pedigree. He claimed his dam was a Canuck, or Canada mare; therefore, some claimed he was not the horse raised by Mr. Berry. His lasting qualities, not only with him, but with his progeny, should be a proof most manifest, that his mother was no Canuck. Being a personal friend of Henry H. Berry, we shall, as briefly as possible, give his own words as he told us in a conversation we had with him on this subject. In the fall of eighteen hundred and thirty-four, Mr. Berry was in the City of New York, and a particular friend of his—Joseph Genung—urged him to buy a very fine mare for breeding purposes that a friend of his owned on Long Island, and, on account of being badly used and driven on the hard roads, her feet had given out and she was offered cheap. Mr. Barry declined to buy her at any price, as he had horses enough.

Mr. Genung said her *blood* made her especially valuable for breeding purposes, as she was by the race-horse Henry, and out of a mare sired by Messenger. The next spring, Mr. Berry was in the city, and found that his friend Genung had bought the mare himself; and when he came to see her, he liked her so well that he did not hesitate a moment in making her his own. This was in the spring of eighteen hundred and thirty-five, and Mr. Berry owned and lived on a large and beautiful farm on Pompton Plains, New Jersey. At the time he bought this mare, she was a beautiful bay animal, somewhat advanced in years, sixteen hands high, with a star and snip in forehead, and both hind feet white above the ankles—a smooth and handsome mare, with a good set of limbs, but bad feet. Mr. Genung was a bachelor, and boarded many years in the family of Mr. Berry's brother, in the city, but died soon after he sold this mare, and thus all hopes of tracing her pedigree more definitely were cut off.

That she was by Henry, and a Messenger mare, there cannot be a shadow of doubt. Mr. Berry thinks she was a thoroughbred. Mr. Ira Coburn, of New York, owned a horse called American Star. He was a bay horse, with star in forehead, fifteen hands high, as round as a rope, with a good set of limbs, pleasant disposition, and could trot very fast; but left no record, as he was used afterwards only as a gentleman's road horse. But, without getting ahead of Mr. Berry's history, we must give it as we received it from him This horse was sent by Mr. Coburn, in the spring of eighteen hundred and thirty-five, to John Riker's tavern, near Little Falls, Passaic County, New Jersey, in charge of Nicholas Smalley, to serve a limited number of mares. Mr. Berry bred this Henry mare, but she failed to get in foal. The next season, Mr. Coburn sent the horse to the same place, but in charge of another groom, who neglected and treated him so badly that Mr. Riker sent word to the owner that he had better take him away. The advice was followed, and the horse returned to New York. Very naturally, Mr. Coburn became heartily disgusted with the stallion business, and meeting Mr. Berry a few days afterwards urged him to take the horse home with him, breed him to as many mares as he liked, and then castrate him—an operation, at that time, in the whole country, performed only by Mr. Berry. This was in eighteen hundred and thirty-six, that Mr. Berry took the horse with him, bred him to his Henry mare, then carried out the instructions of his owner. This mare proved in foal, and dropped this colt in June, eighteen hundred and thirty-seven, which became so famous in Orange County, under the name of his sire, American Star. Mr. Berry says he was disappointed with his colt on its first appearance, both in color and size. However, the colt received but little care or attention—took it as he could catch it—hardly ever under a shelter until three years of age, when he was taken out of the barnyard and broken to harness. There was nothing handsome or stylish about him, but he had a great deal of speed. Mr. Berry ran him a great many quarter and half-mile races, and never had him beaten. At five years of age he served mares at most any price, and was driven to a butcher wagon. He then began to show a fine trotting step. This was in eighteen hundred and forty-two; and the next season he received about the same treatment, and could out-trot any horse in the whole country, and haul that butcher-wagon after him. Mr. Berry often made the remark, that he had the most bottom and best game of any horse he ever saw. In the spring of eighteen hundred and forty-four, he was fixed up a little, and advertised to stand for mares at New Milford and Warwick, Orange County, N. Y.; to insure a mare in foal for *seven* dollars; pedigree given in full; and warranted to haul a wagon on the road a mile in three minutes. From some cause he served but very few mares—in Warwick, we think not any. In August of the same season (eighteen hundred and forty-four), Mr. Berry sold him to Mr. John Blauvelt, a silversmith in New York City, for three hundred and fifty dollars, and a set of single harness. Mr. Blauvelt used him for a road horse, and, as he says, the best he ever rode behind, for pluck, bottom, and speed; but the hard roads and hard drives soon showed the weak points of his dam—his feet giving out, and quarter-cracks making their appearance, he was sent up to Mr. Berry, to be wintered and cured. The next spring he came out all right; but Mr. Blauvelt, apprehending that again the same cause might produce the same effect, traded him off to Cyrus Dubois, of Ulster County, New York, for a grey gelding, at one time owned by Sheriff Westbrook of that county. Dubois had a partner, William Burr, a horseman, now of Hoboken. What time Dubois owned him, we cannot ascertain; but he stood the horse a part of the time in Orange County. Dubois traded him to Jas. Storm, of Hudson, for a bay mare; and after a few days, Storm sold him to Walter Shafer, of Hillsdale, Columbia County, New York; who kept him one or two seasons, then sold him to Edmond Seeley and Hiram Smith, of Goshen, for seven hundred and fifty dollars. This was in the fall of eighteen hundred and forty-nine, and in eighteen hundred and fifty he stood for mares in Goshen, and served fifty-four mares and got forty-five colts, at fifteen dollars per colt. One of these colts we well remember He was called the Randall colt; and, we are very credibly informed, will make a season in this county this year, under the name of his sire, American Star. He has a fast record. In eighteen hundred and fifty-one, he (old Star) made the season in Goshen, at ten dollars to insure—served eighty-seven mares, and got sixty-three colts. In eighteen hundred and fifty-two, at the same place and same price, served ninety-two mares and got sixty-two colts. In eighteen hundred and fifty-three, same place and same price, served forty-nine mares and got thirty-five colts. That fall he was taken to Elmira, Chemung County, New York, and trotted a race against Jupiter. It was a well-contested race, Star winning the sixth heat and race, in 2.45. In eighteen hundred and fifty-four, the next spring, he was taken back to Elmira and stood for mares, served twenty, and got fifteen colts, at twenty dollars per colt. All these colts were mare colts. A very large majority of his get were mares, a fact often spoken of by those who knew. In eighteen hundred and fifty-five he went to Piermont, Rockland County, and served fifty mares and got thirty-five colts, at twenty dollars. In eighteen hundred and fifty-six he went to Mandata,

Illinois, and served thirty mares and got twenty colts, at twenty dollars. In eighteen hundred and fifty-seven he again stood in Goshen, and served sixty-four mares and got fifty-three colts, at twenty dollars. In eighteen hundred and fifty-eight he made the season in Goshen, served fifty-five mares, and got forty-five colts, at twenty dollars. Up to this time the horse had been owned by Edmond Seeley and Hiram Smith, but principally under the control of Uncle Edmond, as we all called him. In the fall or winter of eighteen hundred and fifty-eight, Hiram Smith having found some little fault with the care and treatment the old horse was receiving, Uncle Edmond says, "Here is five dollars, which I will give you to say what you will give or take." The proposition was acceded to, and Uncle Edmond became sole owner of the horse, very unfortunately too, for him; for could Hiram Smith have become sole owner of him, even at that time and age, he would have been a source of great profit to his owner, and would have received that care and attention that a horse of his age most needs; for it is a fact, none could equal Hiram Smith in nursing and taking care of a horse. Another reason why he would have been a source of profit is, the horse had just began to be appreciated, and would, as we think, in Hiram Smith's hands have served mares for five years, and for three of those years would have been patronized at the snug sum of five hundred dollars as the price of service. As it was, Edmond Seeley owned him, and the horse soon began to manifest he had lost a friend. Uncle Edmond, with all his good social qualities, was a poor owner for a horse, and especially for a horse of this horse's age. However, in the spring of eighteen hundred and fifty-nine, American Star stood for service at his owner's stable in Goshen, at twenty-five dollars to insure, and served seventy-one mares and got forty-three colts. In the spring of eighteen hundred and sixty, he again stood in the same stable; but with all of Uncle Edmond's ingenuity —in digging pits for mares to stand in—he failed to serve a quarter of the mares offered; yet he got ten colts at twenty-five dollars. The same fall, Uncle

Edmond gave him away to Theodore Dusenberry, who took him on the farm of Hudson Duryea, near Goshen, where, out in a field, in February, eighteen hundred and sixty-one, he died. His last set were foaled in eighteen hundred and sixty-one: and we simply mention this from the fact that many are offering to sell *Star* Mares foaled in eighteen hundred and sixty-one. And that none may be deceived, we will state that Uncle Edmond owned and had a colt sired by Star, called "SIR HENRY," who made the same season at the same stable, but at a much less price for service. This may be substantiated by any one calling on John Smith, in Goshen, who holds the books of the ten years' service under Uncle Edmond Seeley, and eight years of the time his father Hiram Smith being a partner. AMERICAN STAR passed through many hands, was generally neglected and ill treated; trotted in *his* day, many races, principally on the road or ice, consequently left no very fast record. No horse ever lived that more certainly stamped upon his offspring his own characteristics of *gait, disposition* and *bottom*, than did American

Star. Of his get, you will find a large percentage mares; and many of them may be found on the breeding farms of Orange County, highly appreciated by their owners; and well may be, for they are the mothers of the fastest trotters in the world.

Of his horse colts but a few were kept as stallions. The Randall colt, as he was called, and we have before spoken of, was foaled in eighteen hundred and fifty-one, is a trotter, and a getter of trotters. Magnolia, Sir Henry, and Monitor, all *good stallions* by Star, have been taken out of the county.

BREEDING

AND

MANAGEMENT OF COLTS.

BREEDING.

That a proper knowledge of the laws of breeding is a matter of primary and vast importance, is a generally admitted fact, and requires no argument to prove, as it is only by this means we can maintain the present qualities of our improved breeds, and prevent the race from degenerating, and correct and improve their imperfections. And it is equally true that there are many erroneous views entertained and practiced by many of our farmers. No person should attempt breeding, particularly the horse, without first making it a matter of investigation, patient study, and inquiry. The first axiom we would lay down, says Youatt, is.

that like will produce like, that the progeny will inherit the general or mingled qualities of the parents. There are but few diseases by which either of the parents are affected that the foal does not inherit or show a predisposition to. Broken wind, spavins, ringbones, founders, blindness, roaring and the like, are transmissible, there can be no question, not excepting ill-usage and hard work. These blemishes may not appear in the immediate progeny, but will in the next or more distant generation. From this arises the necessity of some knowledge of both the sire and the dam. The most careless breeders have observed qualities appearing in their stock that belonged to neither sire nor dam, but which belonged to their ancestry further back; such as vicious temper, some peculiar mark, white face or feet. Not only are diseases inherited by the offspring, but the form, spirit, constitution, and temper. *This maxim, however, that "like begets like," is only true in part, as there is a constant tendency to change, arising from differ-

---

*D. J. Bowne, in Patent Office Official Report, 1854.

D

ence in food. Change of climate, or other physical conditions to which they might be exposed, might naturally be expected to produce considerable corresponding modifications in the form, size, color, and coating of animals; as it is well known that cattle generally become very large and fat when reared for many generations on moist, rich soils, where good pasturage abounds, but are distinguished by the shortness of their legs; while on drier situations, where the herbage is sparse, their whole bulk is less, and their limbs more muscular and strong. A country of heaths, or of other innutritious plants, will not produce a horse so large nor so strong as one of plentiful herbage, as is manifested between those reared on bleak mountains and fertile plains, high latitudes and more temperate climes, sandy deserts and watered vales. A change of situation in the one case, after a succession of generations, not only diminishes the size of the animal, but affects the character and form of his body, head, and limbs. Thus, if a London dray horse be conveyed to Arabia, and subjected to the same influences to which the native breed of that country is exposed, in the course of some generations he will present the leading characters of the Arabian horse. On the contrary, if the race thus changed be conveyed again to England, in the course of several generations it will gradually acquire the properties it formerly possessed. This fact would seem to prove that the Arabian horse cannot exist in perfection in any of the northern or western countries of Europe; and that the humidity of the climate, and the influence indirectly arising from that cause, are the principal reasons of this change. Similar instances might be given in reference to the changes which have been observed in the sheep, the goat, and the hog. The former, when subjected to the climate of the West Indies, from Thibet, Spain, or Vermont, where their fleeces are fine, delicate, and soft, after a few years, are entirely covered with rough, coarse hair, resembling that of the goat.

Breeding should be conducted with some definite object in view. There is no greater error than the common remark of some farmers, of some wretched, under-sized, ewe-necked, cat-hammer wreck of a mare, broken-winded, ring-boned, and spavined, "Oh, she will do to raise a colt out of!" She will do! but what will the colt be? It will not be worth the mare's grass, let alone the price of the stallion's service. But it is a good feature that there is a growing anxiety among farmers to raise valuable stock. This is attributable to the fact, that it is not only as cheap to keep a good horse as a bad one, but in reality it is much cheaper. The prime cost is the only difference to be considered; the cost of stable-room, keep and care, is identical; while the wear and tear is infinitely less in the sound, able, useful animal, than in the broken jade. The work which can be done, and the value earned by the one, is in no possible relation to that of the other. The horse bought at the age of four years at three hundred dollars, when he has attained the age of eight, is worth twice the money, either for work or for sale, to the horse that was bought for a third of that price, when he has attained the same age.

What is called *breed* in horses, consists in the superior organization of the nervous and thoracic organs, as compared with the abdominal; the chest is deeper and more capacious; and the brain and nerves more highly developed, – more air is respired, more blood purified, more nervous energy expended. Whilst the heavy cart-horse may be considered to possess the lymphatic temperament, the blood horse may be regarded as the emblem of the nervous and sanguine temperament combined; the latter, however, predominating. When the nervous temperament has the ascendance, the animal will carry but little flesh, but will go till he drops, never seeming to tire. He will, however, take too much out of himself, become thinner, and is what is called a hot horse. When the sanguine temperament greatly prevails, the horse will have great muscular powers, but not much inclination to put them to the stretch. When the lymphatic temperament has superior influence, the animal, though looking fresh and fat, and starting well at first, will soon flag and knock up, and will rather endure the lash than make an extra exertion. It is the happy combination of these three temperaments that make a perfect horse, when severe exertion is demanded. The full development of the abdominal organs is essential, inasmuch as it is through the food that both the muscular system and the nervous energy is furnished If the digestion is weak, the other powers will be inefficiently supplied. The sanguineous organs are needed to furnish the muscular powers, and the nervous system is demanded to furnish the muscles with the requisite energy and capability of endurance. What is called *bottom* in the horse, is neither more nor less than the abundant supply of nervous energy, the muscles being at the same time well developed.

There are two errors commonly committed by persons selecting animals from which to breed. Some pay too much attention to pedigree, and too little to form, spirit, etc. The correct theory is, though form and character is of primary importance, the blood should never be neglected. The great point to be aimed at in a horse for all work, is the combination in the same animal, of maximum of speed, compatible with sufficient size, bone, strength, and solid power, to carry heavy weights, draw large loads, and to secure to the stock the probability of not inheriting deformity or disease from either parent. Breed as much as possible with pure blood, of the right kind; and breed what is technically called, up, not down—that is to say, by breeding the mare to a male of superior, not inferior blood to herself; except where it is desired to breed like to like, as Morgan to Morgan, for the purpose of perpetuating a pure stream of any particular variety which is needful. A half-breed mare should never be put to a half-breed stallion, as, in that case, the product in nine cases out of ten degenerates below the dam; whereas, if she be bred to a thorough-bred stallion, the product will be superior. And the error is, to breed from mares that have become noted for their speed. Some persons will pick up some long-legged, rangy, broken down trotting mare, which could, perhaps, trot her mile in 2.30, thinking to produce something very fine. Nothing can be more ill-judged, as in the majority of instances it is sure to end in disappointment. A mare, with all the best blood in her veins, but without good shape and good points, is not fit for breeding purposes.

And the great and common error in breeding, is to cross a compact dam with a large sire—the object being to increase the size of the offspring above that of the dam—the result is almost sure to end in disappointment. This has been attempted in England, and has proved a failure. The rule deduced from experience is, the dam must be as large or larger than the sire. This *is a historical fact.* The history of breeding shows, that to improve a breed, we must select the best-formed, largest mares, and cross them with medium-sized, compact, muscular stallions.

Size is not the measure of power. Some horses that weigh 900 lbs. will exceed in strength and endurance others of 1,200 lbs., or more; and of those horses that have distinguished themselves as trotters, a large majority have been of medium size. Shortness of legs, with compactness of form, is indispensable to great endurance. The size of the muscles of a horse, other things being equal, determines his power. In selecting a stallion, aim to get one that excels in the point that the mare is deficient in and you wish to avoid in the offspring. Let him exhibit courage and endurance, rather than speed. No one stallion is best adapted to all mares; determine, with a matured judgment, which class of animals your mare is best calculated to produce, whether a roadster, coach horse, or draught animal, and having determined this, use a stallion best calculated to produce the thing reasonably expected, bearing in mind the rule, that "Like will produce like." Breeding, to be successful, must be a matter of study. One point, says Youatt, is absolutely essential, it is "compactness"—as much goodness and strength as possible condensed into a little space.

Next to compactness, the inclination of the shoulder will be regarded. A huge stallion, with upright shoulders, never got a capital hunter or hackney. From him the breeder can obtain nothing but a cart or dray horse, and that, perhaps, spoiled by the opposite form of the mare. On the other hand, an upright shoulder is desirable, if not absolutely necessary, when a mere slow draught-horse is required.

The condition of the stallion is too often overlooked by the most of our farmers. By condition is not meant a high state of fatness, but, on the contrary, it indicates the greatest health and strength, reducing all superfluous fat, bringing the flesh into clear, hard, and powerful muscles. Too many farmers are content with the form and figure of a horse, without regard to condition.

A remarkable case occurred in England, some years since. George the IV. owned, and was in the habit of riding as a hunter, a horse of unqualled excellence. His Majesty caused a few of his mares to be bred to him in the spring, after he had been kept in the highest condition as a hunter throughout the winter, and the produce, on growing up, proved every way worthy of their sire. When His Majesty became seriously engaged in the cares of Government, and therefore relinquished the pleasures of the chase, being desirous to perpetuate the fine qualities of this stock, he ordered the horse to be kept at Windsor for public covering, provided the mares should be of the first quality; and in order to insure a sufficient number of these, directed the head groom to keep him exclusively for such, and to make no charge, with the exception of the customary groom's fee, of half a guinea each. The groom, anxious to pocket as many half guineas as possible, published His Majesty's liberality, and vaunted the qualities of the horse, in order to persuade all he could to avail themselves of the benefit. The result was, the horse being kept without his accustomed exercise and in a state of repletion, and serving upwards of a hundred mares yearly, the stock, although tolerably promising in their early age, shot up into lank, weakly, awkward, leggy, good-for-nothing creatures, to the entire ruin of the horse's character as a sire; until some gentlemen, aware of the cause, took pains to explain it, proving the correctness of their statements by reference to the first of the horse's get, produced under a proper system of breeding, and which were then in their prime, and among the best horses in England.

"In selecting a mare," says Youatt, "it is, perhaps, more difficult to select a good mare to breed from than a good horse, because she should possess somewhat opposite qualities. Her carcass should be long, in order to give room for the growth of the fœtus, and yet with this there should be compactness of form and shortness of leg. In frame, the mare should be so formed as to be capable of carrying and well nourishing her offspring; that is, she should be what is called 'roomy.' There is a formation of the hips which is particularly unfit for breeding purposes, and yet which is sometimes carefully selected, because it is considered elegant; this is the level and straight hip, in which the tail is set on very high, and the end of the haunch bone is nearly on a level with the projection of the hip bone. Nearly the opposite form is the more desirable. She requires such a shape and make as is well adapted for the purpose she is intended for," that is to say, for producing colts of the style and form she is intended to produce. We will add, that she must have four good legs under her, and those legs standing as a foundation on four good, well-shaped, *large* feet, open-heeled, and by no means flat-soled. That she should have a good, lean, bony head, small cased, broad fronted, well set on, upon a high, well carved neck, thin at its junction with the head; high withers, thin shoulders, and above all, long, sloping shoulders. A straight shoulder is an abomination; it renders speed impossible, and gives a rigid, inflexible motion, often producing the bad fault of stumbling. She should be wide-chested, and deep in the heart-place. Her quarters should be strong, well let down, long and sickle-shaped above the hocks. It is better that she go with her hocks somewhat too wide apart than too near together—the former point indicating power, the latter, weakness, of a bad kind. It has been shown that a breed mare may—nay, *should* be considerable longer in the back than one would choose a working horse to be; but if she be particularly so, it is desirable to put her to a particularly short-backed and close-coupled horse. The next thing to be observed by the horse-breeder, in raising stock of any kind, after the blood and form of the mare and the qualities of the stallion, is the temper and condition of the dam. The former, because nothing is more decidedly transmissible in the blood than temper; the second, because, unless she is in good health and vigor, it is impossible that she can produce vigorous and healthy offspring.

The first time a mare is to be covered, it is of the utmost importance that the stallion should be the best that can be procured, as instances have been known where the stallion, having possessed some striking points, the colts of the mare have shown those points for several colts after, though a different stallion was used.

Under no possible circumstances breed from a stallion which has any affection of any kind of the respiratory organs, whether seated in the lungs or in the windpipe; or from one which has any affection of the eyes, unless it be the direct result of an accident, such as a blow, or a puncture, nor even then if the accident, having occurred to one eye, the other has sympathetically followed suit; and, on the other side, we should say, on no account breed from a mare affected in either way, unless she be possessed of some excellencies so extraordinary and countervailing, that, for the sake of preserving the stock, one would be willing to run some risk of having a worthless animal for his own use, in the hope of possibly having one free from the dreaded defect and of superlative excellence.

Previous to sending the mare to the horse, she should be got into the most perfect state of health and condition, by moderate exercise, abundance of good, nutritous food, and warm stabling. It is not desirable that she should be in a pampered state, produced by hot stables or extraordinary clothing; that she should have the short, fine coat, or the blooming and glowing condition of the skin, for which one would look in a race-horse about to contend for a four-mile heat—not that she should be in that wiry form of sinew and steel-like hardiness of muscle, which is only the result of training. Still less desirable is it she should be overloaded with fat, especially that soft fat generated by artificial feeding.

The temper is of great importance, by which must be understood, not that gentleness at grass, which may lead the breeder's family to pet the mare, but such a temper as will serve for the purpose of the rider, and will answer to the stimulus of the voice, whip, or spur. A craven or a rogue is not to be thought of as the mother of a family; and if a mare belong to a breed which is remarkable for refusing to answer to the call of the rider, she should be consigned to any task rather than the stud farm. Sulkiness and savageness are likewise to be avoided, whether in stallion or mare. From the time of covering, to within a few days of the expected period of foaling, the cart-mare may be kept at moderate labor, not only without injury, but with decided advantage. It will then be prudent to release her from work, and keep her near home, and under the frequent inspection of some careful person. When nearly half the time of pregnancy has elapsed, the mare should have a little better food. She should be allowed one or two feeds of grain in the day. This is about the period when they are accustomed to slink their foals, or when abortion occurs; the eye of the owner should, therefore, be frequently upon them. Good feeding and moderate exercise will be the best preventives of this mishap. The mare that has once aborted is liable to a repetition of the accident, and, therefore, should never be suffered to be with other mares between the fourth and fifth months; for such is the power of imagination or of sympathy in the mare, that if one suffers abortion, others in the same pasture will too often share the same fate. Farmers wash, and paint, and tar their stables, to prevent some supposed infection: the infection lies in the imagination.

When the period of parturition is drawing near, she should be watched and shut up during the night in a safe yard, or loose box.

If the mare, whether of the pure or common breed, be thus taken care of, and be in good health while in foal, little danger will attend the act of parturition. If

E

there is false presentation of the fœtus, or difficulty in producing it, it will be better to have recourse to a well-informed practitioner, than to injure the mother by the violent and injurious attempts that are often made to relieve her.

The parturition being over, the mare should be turned into some well-sheltered pasture, with a hovel or shed to run into when she pleases; and if she has foaled early, and grass is scanty, she should have a couple of feeds of grain daily. The breeder may depend upon it that nothing is gained by starving the mother and stinting the foal at this time. It is the most important period of the life of the horse; and if, from false economy, his growth is arrested, his puny form and want of endurance will ever afterwards testify the error that has been committed. The grain should be given in a trough on the ground, that the foal may partake of it with the mother. When the new grass is plentiful, the quantity of feed may gradually be diminished.

The mare will usually be found again at heat at or

before the expiration of nine days from the time of foaling, when, if she is principally kept for breeding purposes, she may be again put to the horse. At the same time, also, if she is used for agricultural purposes, she may go again to work. The foal is at first shut in the stable during the hours of work; but as soon as it acquires sufficient strength to toddle after the mare, and especially when she is at slow work, it will be better for the foal and the dam that they should be together. The work will contribute to the health of the mother; the foal will more frequently draw the milk, and thrive better, and will be hardy and tractable, and gradually familiarized with the objects among which it is afterwards to live. While the mother, however, is thus worked, she and the foal should be well fed; and two feeds of oats at least, should be added to the green food which they get when turned out after their work, and at night.

THE VICES

AND

DISAGREEABLE OR DANGEROUS HABITS OF THE HORSE.

The horse has many excellent qualities; but he has likewise, defects, and these often amount to vices. Some are attributable to natural disposition, but the majority are attributable to bad education and wrong management.

BITING.

This is either the consequence of natural ferocity, or a habit acquired from the foolish and teasing play of grooms and stable boys. Prevention, however, is in the power of every proprietor of horses. While he insists on gentle and humane treatment of cattle, he should systematically forbid this horse-play.

It is seldom that anything can be done in the way of cure. Kindness will aggravate the evil, and no degree of severity will correct it. "I have seen," says Professor Stewart, "biters punished until they tremble in every joint, and were ready to drop, but have never, in any case, known them cured by this treatment, or by any other. The lash is forgotten in an hour, and the horse is as ready and determined to repeat the offence as before. He appears unable to resist the temptation; and, in its worst form, biting is a species of insanity."

Constant and laborious work is often beneficial. Some horses may be over-awed by being very bold. He may be warned by speaking to him. On approaching a horse, hold a whip in his view, ready to let it fall. If you can get hold of his head you are safe; he may then be muzzled, or his head tied to the manger— a long rope may be fastened to the halter, and run through a ring at the head of the stall, and proceed backward to the heel-post; this enables a man to draw the head close up to the ring, and keep it there till the grain or water is delivered, and till the horse can be bridled, muzzled, harnessed, or dressed, as the case may be. He is, of course, to be released after you leave the stall, but the rope remains in place ready for use.

If you can obtain something that is exceedingly disagreeable to the taste of a horse—some bitter herb—saturate a piece of cloth, and wind it around a stick for him to bite; it will often, in connection with kind treatment, have a tendency to break him. A single short cut across the mouth on the instant will sometimes do good.

KICKING.

This, as a vice, is another consequence of the culpable habit of teasing the horse. There is no cure for this vice when it is inveterately established, and he cannot be justified who keeps a kicking horse in his stable. He is never safe, or relied on as being safe. It is foremost in the point of danger, and no treatment will always conquer. An awkward man is always sure to receive injury from a confirmed kicker, and a timid man is never safe. Before the habit is established, a thorn-bush fastened against the partition or post will sometimes effect a cure.

A chain about 20 inches long, strapped in the centre to the horse's foot, is the most effectual remedy known to us.

Kicking in harness is a serious vice. Some horses, by the least annoyance about the rump or quarters, or if the reins get under their tail, they will kick at a most violent rate, endangering everything within their reach. This may be cured by looping up his fore-leg, and teaching him, by several lessons, to draw and walk on three legs; in this position he cannot kick, and in a short time his leg can be taken down, and his propensity for kicking will be found to have subsided; if not, repeat until he is entirely cured. Do not put him in harness the first time his leg is looped up, but first teach him to walk on three legs, without support, out of the harness. Or put on a headstall or bridle, with twisted W, or twisted straight bit, in the mouth of the horse to be cured; then put on a common back-saddle, with thill lugs, or any strap or girth with loops on either side of the horse, is equally good; then buckle a pair of long reins, open in the middle, into the bit, and pass them through the thill lugs or loops, one to each hind leg, above the fetlock joint; there make each rein fast to the leg, allowing sufficient length of rein for your horse to walk or trot, as the operator may think proper. Everything complete, you will have the animal commence the operation of kicking; the first will be a smart kick, and the second lighter, and so on, till your horse cannot be made to kick any more.

Or the following: Take a forked stick, about two feet long, varying a little according to the size of the horse, tie the ends of the fork firmly to each end of the bridle bit, and the other end of the stick to the lower end of the collar, so as to keep the head up. A few days, working in this manner, will commonly suffice for a cure. The man, however, who must come within reach of a kicker, should come as close to him as possible. The blow may thus become a push, and seldom is injurious.

RUNNING AWAY.

The only method which affords any probability of success, is to have him always firmly in hand; and, if he will run away, and the place will admit of it, to give him (sparing neither curb, whip, nor spur,) a great deal more running than he likes. If you wish to stop the horse, if on horseback throw your bridle reins around his neck, if possible, to choke him, or choke him with your arm. If in a wagon, and running away is feared, provide a strong cord with a slipping-noose placed around his neck; if he runs, draw the cord forcibly.

CRIB-BITING.

The causes of crib-biting are various. It is often the result of imitation, idleness, and sometimes by partial starvation. The high fed and spirited horse must be mischievous, if not usefully employed. The crib-biting horse is more subject to colic than other horses, and to a species difficult of treatment and frequently dangerous. This is a bad habit, and very annoying to the owner of a horse. Various remedies have been tried, such as ironing the manger, partitions, etc. I know of no certain cure but an iron muzzle, with bars just wide enough apart to allow the horse to pick up his grain and draw out his hay with his tongue, but not to get hold of anything with his teeth. Common bar soap is a preventive, which is to be rubbed on the edge and outside of the crib, and renewed as often as necessary. If this habit is not broken, it will soon be imitated by every horse in the stable.

WIND-SUCKING.

This bears a close analogy to crib-biting. It arises from the same causes, the same purpose is accomplished, and the same results follow. The horse stands with his neck bent, his lips alternately a little opened and then closed, and a noise is heard as if he were sucking. If we may judge from the same comparative want of condition and the flatulence which we have described under the last head, either some portion of wind enters the stomach, or there is an injurious loss of saliva. This diminishes the value of the horse almost as much as crib-biting; it is as contageous, and it is as inveterate. The only remedies—and they will seldom avail—are tying the head up except when the horse is feeding, or putting on a muzzle with sharp spikes towards the neck, and which will prick him whenever he attempts to rein his head in for the purpose of wind-sucking.—*Youatt.*

CUTTING.

There are some defects in the natural form of the horse, which are the causes of cutting, and which no contrivance will remedy; as, when the legs are placed too near to each other, or when the feet are turned inward or outward. Some horses will cut only when they are fatigued or lame, and old; many colts will cut before they arrive at their full strength. The inside of the fetlock is often bruised by the shoe or the hoof of the opposite foot. Many expedients have been tried to remove this: the inside heel has been raised and lowered, and the outside raised and lowered; and sometimes one operation has succeeded, and sometimes the contrary; and there was no point so involved in obscurity, or so destitute of principles to guide the practitioner. The most successful remedy, and that which, in the great majority of cases supersedes all others, is a shoe of equal thickness from heel to toe, and having but one nail, and that near the toe on the inside of the shoe; care being taken that the shoe shall not extend beyond the edge of the crust, and that the crust shall be rasped a little at the quarters.

NOT LYING DOWN.

It not uncommonly happens that a horse will seldom or never lie down in the stable. He sometimes continues in apparent good health, and feeds and works well; but generally his legs swell, or he becomes fatigued sooner than another horse. They perhaps are afraid of being caught by the halter, or they have already been cast in the night, and do not like to try it again. Such horses should be let loose in a stable at night, or in a large stall without being tied, and furnished with a tempting bed, until the habit of lying down is acquired.

TO PREVENT ROLLING IN THE STALL.

This is a very dangerous habit, and can be prevented only by tying the horse so that he can lie down, but not touch his head to the floor. This is very tiresome to the horse, and hence, if you care enough for his comfort and health, build a narrow platform, eighteen to twenty-four inches in width, slanting at an angle of thirty to forty degrees, so that it will form a pillow for his head and neck; then adjust a rope so that, as he lies down, his head will naturally rest on the platform or pillow. He will not roll unless he can get his head as low as the floor of the stable.

OVER-REACHING OR CLINKING.

An over-reach is a tread upon the heel of the coronet of the fore foot by the shoe of the corresponding hind foot, and is either inflicted by the toe, or by the inner edge of the inside of the shoe.

A writer in the N. E. Farmer, who is a blacksmith, cures overreaching horses, and increases their trotting speed fifteen or twenty seconds per mile, by the following mode of shoeing, which increases the motion of the forward feet, and retards the motion of the hind ones. He makes the toe-caulks very low, standing a very little under, and the shoes set as far backward as convenient on the forward feet, with high heel-caulks, so as to let them roll over as soon as possible. On the hind feet, the heel-caulk is low and the toe-caulk high and projecting forward. Horses shod thus, travel clean, with no click.

PAWING.

Some hot and irritable horses are restless, even in the stable, and paw frequently and violently. Shackles

are the only remedy, with a chain sufficiently long to enable the horse to shift his position; but they must be taken off at night to enable the horse to lie down.
—*Youatt.*

SLIPPING THE HALTER.

This is a trick at which many horses are so clever, that scarcely a night passes without their getting loose. It is a very serious habit, for it enables the horse sometimes to gorge himself with food, to the imminent danger of staggers; or it exposes him, as he wanders about, to be kicked and injured by the other horses; while his restlessness will often keep the whole team awake. If the web of the halter, being first accurately fitted to his neck, is suffered to slip only one way, or a strap is attached to the halter and buckled round the neck, but not sufficiently tight to be of serious inconvenience, the power of slipping the halter will be taken away.—*Youatt.*

TRIPPING

He must be a skillful practitioner, or a mere pretender, who promises to remedy this habit. If it arises from a heavy fore-hand, and the fore-legs being too much under the horse, no one can alter the natural frame of the animal; if it proceeds from tenderness of the foot, grogginess, or old lameness, the ailments are seldom cured. Also, if it is to be traced to habitual carelessness and idleness, no whipping will rouse the drone. A known stumbler should never be ridden or driven by any one who values his safety or his life. A tight hand or a strong bearing-rein are precautions that should not be neglected.

If the stumbler has the foot kept as short, and the toe pared as close as safety will permit, and the shoe is rounded at the toe, or has that shape given to it which it naturally acquires in a fortnight from the peculiar action of such a horse, the animal may not stumble quite so much; or if the disease which produced the habit can be alleviated, some trifling good may be done; but, in almost every case, a stumbler

should be got rid of, or put to slow and heavy work.
—*Youatt.*

PULLING AT THE HALTER.

The following is an effectual method of preventing and curing a horse from pulling at the halter. It should not be applied in a stable unless the animal is watched, as he may throw himself and receive injury:

Put a strong strap or rope around the neck, and another with a ring in it around the pastern of one of the hind feet, and attach a strong rope to the ring, and pass it under a firm strap or cirsingle, buckled loosely around the girth, just back of the shoulder. Continue the rope between the fore legs and through a hole or ring in the manger, or post, where the horse will pull, and then tie it to the strap around the neck, then let him pull "to his heart's content." A few such trials will most likely subdue him. The harder he pulls back the harder his hind foot is pulled forward, and the experimenter will be surprised to see how little the horse can do—he will not be likely to even get his hind foot off the ground.

OPERATIONS, ETC., ETC.

SETONS.

Setons are useful in various cases in abscesses, such as occur in poll evil. In deep fistulous wounds they are indispensable. They promote discharge in the neighborhood of an inflammation. They are made of tow and horse-hair, braided together; or a small cord or a strap of leather may be used. They are inserted by means of an instrument resembling a large needle, either through abscesses, or the base of ulcers with deep sinuses, or between the skin and the muscular or other substances beneath. They are retained there by the ends being tied together, or by a knot at each end. The tape is moved in the wound twice or thrice in the day, and occasionally wetted with spirits of turpentine, or some acrid fluid, in order to increase the inflammation which it produces, or the discharge which is intended to be established.

In inflammation of the chest or intestines, a rowel is preferable to a seton, where the inflammation has long continued, but not intense. Rowels will be serviceable by producing an irritation and discharge. The action of rowels is slower than setons or blistering.

CASTRATION.

Youatt says: "For the common agricultural horse, the age of four or five months will be the most proper time, or, at least, before he is weaned. Few horses are lost when cut at that age.

"If the horse is designed either for the carriage, or for heavy draught, the farmer should not think of castrating him until he is at least a twelvemonth old; and even then the colt should be carefully examined. If he is thin and spare about the neck and shoulders, and low in the withers, he will materially improve by remaining uncut another six months; but if his forequarters are fairly developed at the age of twelve months, the operation should not be delayed, lest he become heavy and gross before, and perhaps has begun too decidedly to have a will of his own.

"No preparation is necessary for the sucking colt, but it may be prudent to bleed and to physic one of more advanced age. In temperate weather he will do much better running in the field than nursed in a close and hot stable. The moderate exercise that he will take in grazing will be preferable to perfect inaction.

"The old method of opening the scrotum (testicle bag) on either side, and cutting off the testicles, and preventing bleeding by a temporary compression of the vessels while they are seared with a hot iron, must not, perhaps, be abandoned.

"Another method of castration is by *Torsion*. An incision is made into the scrotum, and the *vas diferens* is exposed and divided. The artery is then seized by a pair of forceps, contrived for the purpose, and twisted six or seven times round. It retracts without untwisting the coils, and bleeding ceases. The most painful part of the operation—the operation of the firing-iron or the clams—is avoided, and the wound readily heals."

BLEEDING.

This operation is performed with a fleam or a lancet. The first is the common instrument, except in skillful hands. The lancet, however, has a more surgical appearance, and will be adopted by the veterinary practitioner. A bloodstick is used to strike the fleam into the vein. This is sometimes done with too great violence, and the opposite side of the coat of the vein is wounded. Bad cases of inflammation have resulted from this. If the fist is doubled, and the fleam is sharp, and is struck with sufficient force with the lower part of the hand, the bloodstick may be dispensed with.

For general bleeding the jugular vein is selected. The horse is blindfolded on the side on which he is to be bled, or his head turned well away. The hair is smoothed along the course of the vein with the moistened finger; then, with the third and little finger of the left hand, which holds the fleam, pressure is made on the vein sufficient to bring it fairly into view, but not to swell it too much, for, then presenting a rounded surface, it would be apt to roll or slip under the blow. The point to be selected is about two inches below the union of the two portions of the jugular at the angle of the jaw. The fleam is to be placed in a direct line with the course of the vein, and over the precise centre of the vein, as close to it as possible, but its point not absolutely touching the vein. A sharp rap with the hand on that part of the back of the fleam immediately over the blade will cut through the vein, and the blood will flow. A fleam with a large blade should always be preferred. A quantity of blood drawn speedily will also have far more effect on the system than double the weight slowly taken, while the wound will heal just as readily as if made by a smaller instrument. A slight pressure, if the incision has been large enough and straight, and in the middle of the vein, will cause the blood to flow sufficiently fast; or, the finger being introduced into the mouth between the tushes and the grinders, and gently moved about, will keep the mouth in motion, and hasten the rapidity of the stream by the action and pressure of the neighboring muscles

When sufficient blood has been taken, the edges of the wound should be brought closely and exactly together, and kept together by a small, sharp pin being passed through them. Round this a little tow should be wrapped, so as to cover the whole of the incision; and the head of the horse should be tied up for several hours to prevent his rubbing the part against the manger. In bringing the edges of the wound together and introducing the pin, care should be taken not to draw the skin too much from the neck, otherwise blood will insinuate itself between it and the muscles beneath, and cause an unsightly and sometimes troublesome swelling.

The blood should be received into a vessel, the dimensions of which are exactly known, so that the operator may be able to calculate at every period of the bleeding the quantity that is extracted. Care, likewise, should be taken that the blood flows in a regular stream into the centre of the vessel, for if it is suffered to trickle down the sides it will not afterwards undergo those changes by which we partially judge of the extent of inflammation. The pulse, however, and the symptoms of the case collectively, will form a better criterion than any change in the blood. Twenty-four hours after the operation the edges of the wound will have united, and the pin should be withdrawn. When the bleeding is to be repeated, if more than three or four hours have elapsed, it will be better to make a fresh incision rather than to open the old wound.

In local inflammation, blood may be taken from any of the superficial veins. In supposed affection of the shoulder, or of the fore-leg or foot, the *plate* vein, which comes from the inside of the arm, and runs upwards directly in front of it towards the jugular, may be opened. In affections of the hind extremity, blood is sometimes extracted from the *saphæna*, or thigh-vein, which runs across the inside of the thigh. In foot cases it may be taken from the coronet, or, much more safely, from the toe; not by cutting out a piece of the sole at the toe of the frog—which sometimes causes a wound difficult to heal, and followed by festering and even by canker—but cutting down with a fine drawing-knife, called a searcher, at the union between the crust and the sole at the very toe until the blood flows, and, if necessary, encouraging its discharge by dipping the foot in warm water. The mesh-work of both arteries and veins will be here divided, and blood is generally obtained in any quantity that may be needed. The bleeding may be stopped with the greatest ease, by placing a bit of tow in the little groove that has been cut, and tacking the shoe over it.*—*Youatt.*

---

*A great improvement has lately been introduced in the method of arresting arterial hermorrhage. The operation is very simple, and, with common care, successful. The instrument is a pair of artery forceps, with rather sharper teeth than the common forceps, and the blades held close by a slide. The vessel is laid bare, detached from the cellular substance around it, and the artery then grasped by the forceps, the instrument deviating a very little from the line of the artery. The vessel is now divided close to the forceps, and behind them, and the forceps are twisted four or five times round. The forceps are then loosened, and, generally speaking, not more than a drop or two of blood will have been lost. This meteod of arresting bleeding has been applied by several scientific and benevolent men with almost constant success. It has been readily and effectually practiced in docking, and patients have escaped much torture,

THE PULSE.

The pulse is a very useful assistant to the veterinary surgeon, whose patients cannot describe either the seat or degree of ailment or pain. In a state of health the heart beats in a horse about thirty-six times a minute. This is said to be the *standard* pulse—the pulse of health. Where it beats naturally there can be little materially wrong. The most convenient place to feel the pulse is at the lower jaw, a little behind the spot where the sub-maxillary artery and vein, and the parotid duct, come from under the jaw. There the number of pulsations will be easily counted, and the character of the pulse, a matter of fully equal importance, will be clearly ascertained.

When the pulse reaches fifty or fifty-five, some degree of fever may be apprehended, and proper pre-

---

and tetanus lost many a victim. The forceps have been introduced, and with much success, in castration, and thus the principal danger of that operation, as well as the most painful part of it, is removed. The colt will be a fair subject for this experiment. On the sheep and the calf it may be readily performed, and the operator will have the pleasing consciousness of rescuing many a poor animal from the unnecessary infliction of torture.—*Spooner.*

caution should be taken. Seventy or seventy-five will indicate a dangerous state, and put the owner and the surgeon a little on the alert. Few horses long survive a pulse of one hundred, for, by this excessive action, the energies of nature are speedily worn out. Some things should be taken into account in forming our conclusion of the pulse. Exercise, a warm stable, and fear will wonderfully increase the number of pulsations.

If a *quick* pulse indicate irritation and fever, a *slow* pulse will likewise characterize diseases of an opposite description. It accompanies the sleepy stage of staggers, and every malady connected with deficiency of nervous energy.

The heart may be excited to more frequent and more violent action. It may contract more powerfully upon the blood, which will be driven with greater force through the arteries, and the expansion of the vessels will be greater and more sudden. Then we have the *hard* pulse—the sure indicator of considerable fever, and calling for the immediate and free use of the lancet.

Sometimes the pulse may be hard and jerking, and yet *small*. The stream, though forcible, is not great. The practitioner knows that this indicates a dangerous state of disease. It is an almost invariable accompaniment of inflammation of the bowels.

A *weak* pulse, when the arterial stream flows slowly, is caused by the feeble action of the heart. It is the reverse of fever, and expressive of debility.

The *oppressed* pulse is when the arteries seem to be fully distended with blood. There is obstruction somewhere, and the action of the heart can hardly force the stream along, or communicate pulsation to the current.

The state of the pulse should be carefully regarded during bleeding. The most experienced practitioner cannot tell what quantity of blood must be abstracted in order to produce the desired effect. The change of the pulse can alone indicate when the object is accomplished; therefore, the operator should have his finger on the artery during the act of breeding, and, comparatively regardless of the quantity, continue to take blood until, in inflammation of the lungs, the oppressed pulse becomes fuller and more distinct, or the strong pulse of considerable fever is evidently softer, or the animal exhibits symptoms of faintness.

It is important to distinguish between the pulse of fever and that of inflammation. We may have a pulse of the greatest rapidity, as in influenza, and yet no one part of the body much inflamed. We have known the pulse of the horse more than tripled, and the animal still recover; and, on the other hand, in cases of inflammation, a pulse of sixty has betokened great danger, and, in some cases, has been succeeded by death.

CLYSTERS.

The principal art of administering a clyster consists in not frightening the horse. The pipe, well oiled, should be very gently introduced, and the fluid not too hastily thrown into the intestine, its heat being as nearly as possible that of the intestine, or about 96° of Fahrenheit's thermometer.

These are useful in hastening the evacuation of the bowels when the disease requires their speedy action.

Two ounces of soft or yellow soap, dissolved in a gallon of warm water, will form a useful aperient clyster. For a more active aperient, half a pound of Epsom salts, or even of common salt, may be dissolved in the same quantity of water. A stronger injection, but not to be used if much purgative medicine has been previously given, may be composed of an ounce of Barbadoes aloes, dissolved in two or three quarts of warm water. If nothing else can be procured, warm water may be employed.

In cases of over-purging, or inflammation of the bowels, the injection must be of a soothing nature. It may consist of gruel alone, or, if the purging is considerable, and difficult to stop, the gruel must be thicker, and four ounces of prepared, or powdered chalk, well mixed with or suspended in it, with two scruples or a drachm of powdered opium.

No oil should enter into the composition of a

clyster, except that linseed oil may be used for the expulsion of ascarides, or needle-worms

In epidemic catarrh, when the horse sometimes obstinately refuses to eat or to drink, his strength may be supported by nourishing clysters; but they should consist of thick gruel only, and not more than a quart should be administered at once.

TRACHEOTOMY.

" This operation consists in making an opening into the windpipe to admit air to the lungs, when the natural passage is obstructed by foreign bodies, or when its calibre is lessened by tumefaction occasioned by disease. In severe cases of laryngitis, strangles, and their kindred diseases, when the patient seems almost suffocated, tracheotomy should be immediately performed. In performing the operation, we select a spot about six inches below the throat, in front of the neck, and over the region of the windpipe; an incision is to be made with a common penknife (in lieu of a better instrument), to the extent of two or three inches, in a downward direction, so as to lay bare the trachea; having exposed space sufficient, a circular piece between two rings, corresponding to the size of the tube, is to be cut out, and a short tube inserted, which can be confined in position by means of tape passed around the neck. When the obstruction is removed, or the fances restored to their natural state, remove the tube, bring the edges of the integuments together, and sew them up."—*Dr. Dadd.*

PHYSICING.

This is often necessary, but it has injured the constitution and destroyed thousands of animals, when unnecessarily or improperly resorted to. When the horse comes from grass to dry feed, or from the open air to the heated stable, and is becoming too fat, or has surfeit, or grease, or mange, or is out of condition from inactivity of the digestive organs, a dose of physic is serviceable; but the physicing of all horses, and the too frequent method of exercising the animal when under the operation of physic, cannot be too strongly condemned.

A horse should be carefully prepared for the action of physic. Mashes should be given until the dung becomes softened. Five drachms of aloes, given when the dung has thus been softened, will act much more effectually and much more safely then seven drachms when the lower intestines are obstructed by hardened dung.

On the day on which the physic is given, the horse should have exercise; but after the physic begins to work, he should not be moved from his stall.

A little hay may be put into the rack. As much mash should be given as the horse will eat, and as much water, with the coldness of it taken off, as he will drink. If he refuses to drink warm water, it is better that he should have it cold than to continue without taking any fluid; but, in such case, he should not be suffered to take more than a quart at a time, with an interval of at least an hour between each draught. The cleansing powder will be found an excellent physic. The Barbadoes aloes, although sometimes very dear, should alone be used. The dose, with a horse properly prepared, will vary from four to seven drachms.

DISEASES.

STRANGLES OR HORSE DISTEMPER.

This disease is principally incident to young horses, usually appearing between the fourth and fifth year, and oftener in the spring than at any other time. It occasionally attacks old animals. Few horses escape its attack; but, the disease having passed over, the animal is free from it for the remainder of his life. This disease is usually considered contagious, but we are not clear upon this point; however, it will be well to separate the patient from healthy animals. This we would recommend in all cases of catarrhal affection.

SYMPTOMS.—It is generally preceded by cough, with a discharge from the nostrils of a yellowish color, mixed with pus, generally without smell; the membrane of the nose intensely red, a swelling under the throat which increases, accompanied by a fever, a disinclination to eat, and a considerable thirst, but after a gulp or two the horse ceases to drink. In attempting to swallow, a convulsive cough comes on, which threatens to suffocate the animal and the mouth is hot and tongue coated with white fur. The tumor under the jaw and about the centre of the channel soon fills the whole space, and is evidently one uniform body, and may thus be distinguished from glanders or the enlarged glands of catarrh. In a few days it becomes more prominent and soft, and evidently contains a fluid. This rapidly increases, the tumor bursts, and a great quantity of pus is discharged. As soon as the tumor has broken, the cough subsides, and the horse speedily mends, although some degree of weakness may hang about him for considerable time.

TREATMENT.—As soon as the tumor under the jaw is decidedly apparent, the part should be actively blistered. It should be washed off as soon as it rises, and if repeated in a day or two, this will abate the internal inflammation and soreness of the throat, and promote the suppurative process. When the glands remain hard, and do not suppurate, it may lead to glanders, in which case the use of Iodine Ointment as an outward application, and hydriodate of potash in daily doses of ten to forty grains, combined with tonics, will be found useful as an internal application.

As soon as the swelling is soft on its summit, and evidently contains matter, it should be freely and deeply lanced, after which apply a linseed poultice. If the incision is deep and large enough, no second collection of matter will be formed; and that which is already there may be suffered to run out slowly, all pressure with the fingers being avoided. The part should be kept clean. The appetite will return with the opening of the abscess. Bran-mashes, or fresh-cut grass should be liberally supplied, which will not only afford sufficient nourishment to recruit the strength of the animal, but keep the bowels gently open. If the weakness is not great, no further medicine will be wanted, except a dose of mild physic, in order to prevent the swellings or eruptions which sometimes succeed to strangles. In cases of debility, a small quantity of tonic medicine, as camomile, gentian, or ginger may be administered.

No. 2. Homœopathic treatment: Fever symptoms, Aconite, 10 to 15 drops, once an hour; when allayed. arsenicum, 12 to 15 drops.

BLISTERING

The principle on which they act is, that two intense inflammations cannot exist in neighboring parts at the same time; they also increase the action of contiguous vessels. Inflammation should be met promptly with blistering. Old enlargements and swellings can be removed by milder stimulants, such as *sweating down* the part to be blistered. The hair should be shaved, and the ointment thoroughly rubbed in. Care should be taken that the horse cannot hurt himself. After twenty-four hours, a little olive or neat's foot oil should be applied over the blister. Apply the oil, morning and night, until the scab peels off. Where there is a tendency to grease, blistering is dangerous. In the winter, care should be used that the horse does not take cold in the part blistered.

INFLAMMATION OF THE KIDNEYS.

SYMPTOMS.—A constant desire to void urine, although only passed in small quantities, highly colored, and sometimes tinged with blood, though more generally quite natural. There is usually a peculiar stiffness in the hind extremities, especially when the horse is made to describe a circle. Pressure on the loins elicit symptoms of pain, and the pulse and respirations denote febrile symptoms.

The treatment will only vary from that of inflammation of other parts by a consideration of the peculiarity of the organ affected. Bleeding may be promptly resorted to. An active purge should next be administered, and a counter inflammation excited as nearly as possible to the seat of disease. For this purpose the loins should be fomented with hot water, or covered with a mustard poultice—the horse should be warmly clothed, and no diuretic should be given internally. One of the best applications to the loins is a fresh sheep skin, the skin side inwards. This will very soon cause and keep up a considerable perspiration, which may be continued by means of a fresh skin in the course of twelve hours. With regard to internal medicines, one of the best sedatives is the white hellebore, in doses of a scruple twice a day. The bowels should be opened by means of an aperient draught, and abundance of linseed tea should be given so as to sheath the irritated parts. The patient should be warmly clothed, his legs well bandaged, and plenty of water offered to him. The food should be carefully examined, and anything that could have excited, or that may prolong the irritation, carefully removed.

INFLAMMATION OF THE BLADDER.

This is a very rare but exceedingly dangerous disease. There are two varieties of this disease,—

inflammation of the body of the bladder, and of its neck. The symptoms are nearly the same as with those of inflammation of the kidney, except that there is rarely a total suppression of urine, and there is heat felt in the rectum over the situation of the bladder. The causes are, the presence of some acrid or irritant matter in the urine, or of calculus or stone in the bladder. In inflammation of the neck of the bladder, there is the same frequent voiding of urine in small quantities, generally appearing in an advanced stage of the disease, and often ending in almost total suppression. There is this circumstance which can never be mistaken: the bladder is distended with urine, and can be distinctly felt under the rectum. It is spasm of the part, closing the neck of the bladder so powerfully that the contraction of the bladder and the pressure of the muscles are unable to force out the urine.

The treatment in this case will be the same as in inflammation of the kidneys, except that it is of more consequence that the animal should drink freely of water or thin gruel.

The irritation being great, it is almost impossible to keep any soothing application in the bladder, the contents of which are being continually ejected; recourse, therefore, must be had to very copious bleeding, so as to endeavor to check the inflammation which exists, as well as to assuage the irritation, which forbids local measures. It will assist, to administer calomel conbined with opium and tartarized antimony, to scruples of each being given three times a day. The same means may be adopted when inflammation attacks the neck of the bladder, and the spasm prevents its evacuation. The bladder of a mare can be easily evacuated by means of a catheter; and, by the aid of the elastic and flexible catheter, the bladder of the gelding can also be discharged, though the operation requires some tact and skill.

INFLAMMATION OF THE STOMACH AND BOWELS.

There are two varities of this malady. The first is inflammation of the external coats of the intestines, called *peritonitis*, accompanied by considerable fever, and usually costiveness. The second is that of the internal or mucous coat, called *enteritis*.

The muscular coat is that which is oftenest affected. Inflammation of the external coats of the stomach, whether the peritoneal or muscular, or both, is a very frequent and fatal disease. It speedily runs its course, and it is of great consequence that its early symptoms should be known.

The causes of *peritonitis* are both numerous and various. We have seen that colic may give rise to it. Constipation may be viewed in the light both of cause and effect in its relation to it. Collected hardened fæces must naturally, not only of themselves, be irritative, but obstructive and subersive of the functions of the bowels, and in either one or the other ways may lay the foundation for an attack of inflammation. Certain kinds of indigestible food, calculous bodies, irritating matter of any sort, within the bowels, may cause an inflammation of them. Obstruction of any of their passages—whether it be from the lodgment and immovableness of the matters they contain, or from entanglement of the intestines, or intus-susception—must in the end occasion inflammation. Over-fatigue, and consequent excessive irritation in the bowels, will bring it on.

SYMPTOMS.—There is some analogy between the symptoms of this disease and colic; there is, however, one marked feature of the case which enables us to diagnose the disease with some degree of certainty, for when inflamation has fairly set in there is little, if any, remission of pain; whereas, in colic, the pains are of a spasmodic character, so that the animal at times is quite easy. The pulse, in inflammation of the bowels, is small, firm, and quick, increasing in beat as the disease increases in intensity.

"The next stage borders on delirium. The eye acquires a wild, haggard, unnatural stare—the pupil dilates—his heedless and dreadful throes render approach to him quite perilous. He is an object not only of compassion but of apprehension, and seems fast hurrying to his end; when, all at once, in the midst of agonizing torments, he stands quiet, as though every pain had left him, and he were going to recover. His breathing becomes tranquilized—his pulse sunk beyond all conception—his body bedewed with a cold, clammy sweat—he is in a tremor from head to foot, and about the legs and ears has even a death-like feel. The mouth feels deadly chill, the lips drop pendulous, and the eye seems unconscious of objects: in fine, death, not recovery, is at hand. Mortification has seized the inflamed bowel—pain can no longer be felt in that which, a few minutes ago, was the seat of exquisite suffering. He again becomes convulsed, and in a few more struggles, less violent than the former, he expires."

TREATMENT.—The treatment should be prompt and energetic. The first and most powerful means of cure will be bleeding. From six to eight quarts of blood should be abstracted as soon as possible; and the bleeding repeated if the pain is not relieved and the pulse has not become rounder and fuller. Weakness is the consequence of the violent inflammation of these parts, and if that inflammation is subdued by the loss of blood the weakness will disappear. The bleeding should be effected on the first appearance of the disease.

A strong solution of aloes should immediately follow the bleeding, but guarded by opium. This should be quickly followed by back-raking, and ejections consisting of warm water, or very thin gruel, in which Epsom salts or aloes have been dissolved; and too much fluid can scarcely be thrown up. If the common ox-bladder and pipe is used, it should be frequently replenished. The horse should likewise be encouraged to drink plentifully of warm water or thin gruel; and draughts, each containing a couple of drachms of dissolved aloes, with a little opium, should be given every six hours, until the bowels are freely opened.

Dr. Dadd recommends a method of treatment quite different from the above. He is very much opposed to blood-letting in all cases. That bleeding is efficacious in this and other diseases is certain, but we are not certain that the same results cannot be attained by milder and other remedies. There has been a reform, of late years, in the human practice with good results, and why cannot the same ends be accomplished in the veterinary practice? We would recommend a careful perusal of Dr. Dadd, in "Modern Horse Doctor," on this disease.

COLIC.

In nine cases out of ten, colic is the result of impaired digestive organs. The drinking of cold water when the horse is heated is a very sure origin of violent spasm in the horse. Hard water is very apt to produce this effect. Colic will sometimes follow the exposure of a horse to the cold air or a cold wind after strong exercise. Green feed, although, generally speaking, most beneficial to the horse, yet, given in too large a quantity, or when he is hot, will frequently produce gripes. Doses of aloes, both large and small, are not unfrequent causes of colic.

SYMPTOMS.—It is of much importance to distinguish between spasmodic colic and inflammation of the bowels, for the symptoms have considerable resemblance, although the mode of treatment should be very different.

The attack of colic is usually very sudden. The horse begins to shift his posture, look around at his flanks, paw violently, strike his belly with his feet, and crouch in a peculiar manner, advancing his hind limbs under him; he will then suddenly lie, or, rather fall down, and balance himself upon his back, with his feet resting on his belly. The pain now seems to cease for a little while, and he gets up and shakes himself, and begins to feed; the respite, however, is but short, the spasm returns more violently—every indication of pain is increased—he heaves at the flanks, breaks out into a profuse perspiration, and throws himself more recklessly about. In the space of an hour or two, either the spasms begins to relax, and the remissions are of longer duration, or the torture is augmented at every paroxysm; the intervals of ease are fewer and less marked, and inflammation and death supervene. The pulse is but little affected at the commencement, but it soon becomes frequent and contracted, and at length is scarcely perceptible.

TREATMENT.—Take powdered grains of paradise, 1 tea-spoonful; powdered caraway, ¼ tea-spoonful; oil of peppermint, 20 drops; powdered slippery elm, 1 table-spoonful; hot water, 1 pint; mixed together and given from a bottle. An injection of common soap-suds thrown into the rectum. Peppermint tea alone will sometimes afford relief and a perfect cure. Saleratus is a favorite remedy with many, but it should not be mixed with milk or molasses, as is often done.

If the animal labors under pyloric obstruction, the following is a good preparation: Carbonate ammonia, 1 drachm; tincture of ginger, 1 ounce; water, 1 pint. Mix, and drench the horse.

SCOURS AND CONSTIPATION IN COLTS.

The principal cause of this disease is the want of proper management of the mother. It is a law of nature, that whatever affects the bowels of the mother will also affect the colt through the milk it derives, though more seriously; for the colt must now, and until it be able to masticate food, depend altogether on the parent's milk, and the latter cannot furnish it in sufficient quantities unless kept on generous food.

TREATMENT.—Our first duty is to attend to the wants of the mother—establish her health if it be impaired.

Stock raisers might learn a lesson from nurses who attend human parturients—they give the old-fashioned dose of castor oil understandingly, knowing from long experience that it operates both on the mother and child.

The milk of the mother, immediately after parturition, is the best kind of medicine to regulate the secretions and excretions of the offspring, and it generally has the desired effect. There may, however, be cases where, in consequence of exposure, the foal may have diarrhœa, if so, it must be placed in a warm situation. Perhaps all that will now be needed for the cure is some warm ginger, or caraway tea; and a little of either of these simple articles pulverized, may, with advantage, be given to the mother in her food. If the mother is fat, and has not had sufficient exercise previous to parturition, we are not to be in a hurry to stop the discharge, but merely to hold it in check. If in poor condition, and still losing flesh, then, in addition, give of tonic, and give freely of gruel made of wheat flour; and while it continues the foal should not depend altogether on his dam for sustenance, but might have a daily allowance of boiled cow's milk, cooled to about the temperature of milk when drawn. Hay tea, to which a small quantity of cow's milk may be added, is an excellent drink for the young foal in the absence of its mother's milk. Try it, reader, on your calves also, if you have occasion.

The following astringent drinks for colts is efficacious, viz.: Angelica root, 1 ounce; cranesbill, 2 ozs. bayberry bark, ½ ounce; African ginger, ½ ounce. Pour on the above ingredients 2 quarts of boiling water; set them aside for a few hours. Dose: Half a pint every four hours until the disease is checked. If the discharges are fetid, add to each dose half a table-spoonful of finely-pulverized charcoal; and if the foal be weak and in poor condition, allow it hay tea, thickened with oatmeal.

As regards costiveness, green food and scalded shorts are the *antidotes*, and the mother will partake of either with relish. Some of the former, if the season permits, should be cut and placed before her soon after labor. If the articles fail to have the desired effect, a dose of aperient medicine—caster oil, or salts—should be given.

DIARRHŒA.

This is quite a common disease among horses. There is a kind, however, among grass-eaters, that is beneficial rather than otherwise, if it does not continue for any length of time. Diarrhœa is the effect of an irritable or congested state of the muscous membrane of the intestines; often produced by improper articles, or over-doses of physic, by over-exertion and perspiration suddenly checked by exposure to cold winds, &c.

SYMPTOMS.—The symptoms are—he frequently looks round at his flanks, his breathing is laborious, and the pulse is quick and small;. the mouth is hot, and the legs and ears are warm.

TREATMENT.—If it proceeds from the feed, change of diet will generally be sufficient. Unless the purging is excessive, and the pain and distress great, the surgeon should hesitate at giving any astringent medicine at first; but administer gruel, thin starch, or arrowroot, by the mouth and by clyster, and remove all hay and corn, and particularly green feed. If, however, twelve hours have passed, and the purging and the pain are undiminished, continue the gruel, adding to it chalk, catechu, and opium, repeated every six hours. As soon as the purging begins to subside, the astringent medicine should be lessened in quantity, and gradually discontinued. The horse should be warmly clothed, and placed in a comfortable stable, and his legs should be hand-rubbed and bandaged. Bayberry bark and charcoal are powerful astringents.

If the disease depends upon deranged digestive

function, the liver included, give a few doses of the following: Powdered goldenseal, 2 ounces; powdered ginger, 1 ounce; salt, 1 ounce. Dose, half an ounce twice a day.

INDIGESTION.

The causes of indigestion are numerous—too little or too much of food, water, or work; bad ventilation, exposure, poisons, damaged or highly nutritious food, or working the animal on a full stomach, are all operative in producing indigestion in acute or chronic forms.

SYMPTOMS.—The excrement is very variable in color and consistence, often hard and covered with slime; at other times soft, when the presence of intestinal parasites can be detected. The urine is scanty, and either colored or thickened with foreign material. The animal is generally cross and irritable, and leaves the stable at working-time very unwillingly. He requires considerable urging while travelling, and, of course, is incapacitated to perform his usual work.

TREATMENT.—First, if possible, remove the cause.

If the animal has been fed on dry food, let him have a mixture of boiled oats, shorts, and carrots, well seasoned with salt, to which add daily half a tablespoonful of white mustard-seed; ¼ pint of pale brandy to 4 ounces of fine salt—dose, a wine-glass, in oatmeal gruel, night and morning, just before meals. The animal must not be permitted to spend half his time eating. Attention must also be paid to the water which the animal drinks. Throw a handful of pulverized charcoal, daily, into the water-trough. This will improve the very worst kind.

WARTS.

These excrescences, arising from the cuticular covering of the skin, are sometimes very annoying to horses, especially when occurring about the eye, sheath, penis, or on parts which come in contact with the harness.

TREATMENT.—A wart having a broad base should be treated in the following manner: Take a common suture needle, and arm it with a double ligature—each ligature is to be composed of three threads of saddler's twine, well waxed; pass the needle through the centre of the wart, close down to the skin; tie each half separately with a *surgeon's knot*, as tight as possible; cut the end off pretty close to the knot, and in the course of a short time the whole will drop off. A wart having a small circumscribed pedicel may be removed in the same way, by tying a *single* ligature round its base. If the exposed surface should not heal readily, moisten it occasionally with tincture of aloes and myrrh; and if they show a disposition to ulcerate, sprinkle them with powdered charcoal and blood-root, equal parts. Warts about the sheath or penis should be removed by incision. To do this, we often have to cast the animal—the consequent hemorrhage to be arrested with tincture of muriate of iron, or styptic.

SLOBBERING.

This complaint is quite common in rural districts, where clover is used as a pasture. Lobelia or tobacco will produce the same results. This is caused by irritation, the article coming in direct contact with highly sensitive secretary surfaces, which always pour out their fluids on the application of an irritant, so long as it remains an irritant, and provided the parts retain their normal sensibility, or through the medium of absorbents; thus, calomel will cause the salivatory gland to secrete and pour forth an amount of fluid almost incredible. A horse will secrete more than one and a half gallons of fluid per hour. The sharp edges of a worn-down tooth, or a tooth in a state of ulceration, may give rise to profuse salivation; then again. a rough bit, and a hard master, may be set down among the direct causes of this complaint. Indifferent fodder of any kind, and impaired digestive organs, are apt to produce augmented salivary secretion.

TREATMENT.—The causes should be sought for, and, if practicable, removed. This may of itself produce relief. If the trouble can be traced to a carous tooth, let it be extracted; or should the edges of a tooth irritate the inside of the cheek, apply the tooth-rasp, and make all smooth. If any irritation exists about the glands of the throat and mouth, apply a stimulating application to them, composed of hartshorn and olive oil. If something noxious in the food, give the following :—

Powdered bayberry bark, powdered myrrh, powdered goldenseal, powdered ginger, powdered sulphur, of each 1 ounce. Mix, divide the mass into eight parts, and mix one in fine feed; or gargles, composed of decoction of witch hazel, bayberry bark, tincture gum catechu, and a solution of alum, either of which is good, when an astringent is indicated.

No. 2. Mix a table-spoonful of sulphur in salt, give once or twice a week.

No. 3. Burdock leaves are said to effect a cure. Horses will not eat them only when they are troubled with slobbers, and thus eradicate two evils at one time.

SPAVIN.

This is a very common and formidable disease of the hock, and we have but little to offer by way of cure, and the majority of cases may be pronounced incurable; the lameness may be in part or entirely cured, but the spavin cannot be radically removed. The principal cause of the disease may be found in breeding from old, broken down, spavin mares and worthless studs; but the exciting or immediate cause is strain, injury, over-work, &c.

The weight and concussion being thrown principally on the inner splent-bone, produce inflammation of the cartilagenous substance that unites it to the shank-bone. In consequence of it, the cartilage is absorbed and bone deposited; the union between the splent-bone and the shank becomes bony, instead of cartilagenous; the degree of elastic action between them is destroyed, and there is formed a splent of the hind leg. The disposition to form bony matter having commenced, bone continues to be deposited, and it generally appears in the form of a tumor, where the head of the splent-bone is united with the shank, and in front of that union. This is called bone spavin. Inflammation of the ligaments of any of the small bones of the hock, proceeding to bony tumor, would equally class under the name of spavin; but, commonly, the disease commences on the precise spot that has been described.

SYMPTOMS.—While spavin is forming there is generally lameness, and sometimes very great, but not entirely to unfit him for work. The lameness sometimes abates and entirely disappears, by a little exercise; but when the membrane of the bone has accommodated itself to the tumor that extended it, lameness subsides or disappears, or depends upon the degree which the bony deposit interfered with the motion of the joint. Sometimes there is no tumor; then, if a sort of regular lameness has existed for some months, referable to no other joint than the hock, and the difficulty has of late gradually increased, so that the joint appears stiff, the critter is there, after which we may expect to observe a tumor on the inside of the hock. A tumor once formed in the region already referred to needs no *wise man* to point it out; it can be both seen and felt; and this, accompanied with hock lameness and ligamentary tumefaction, is the symptom of spavin in its *exostotic* stage.

TREATMENT.—The remedy in the early stage, cold water and refrigerated lotions; in the latter stages, strong infusion of bayberry bark; and lastly, brandy and salt, perseveringly applied. Congestion may be treated in the same manner, aided by friction.

The horse, as soon as the lameness or dry signs of the disease are perceptible, should have rest, and cooling applications should be applied. Dr. Dadd says —Our usual remedy in the early stage is muriatic acid, 4 ounces; water, 2 quarts; tincture of bloodroot, 6 ounces; applied daily by means of a sponge as follows: Take a piece of sponge, slightly concave, corresponding, as nearly as possible, to the form and size of the hock; by means of a few stitches, affix two pieces of tape, or linen, so as to form an X; each piece must be long enough to encircle the joint two or three times. After dipping the sponge in the mixture, it must be applied to the inside of the hock, and there secured, and afterwards kept constantly moist. Dr.

Spooner says—If any external inflammation is present we cannot do better than commence by abstracting blood from the vein above, and use cooling applications to the hock, after which we may resort to the blister, or seton.

RINGBONE.

Ringbone is a deposit of bony matter in one of the pasterns, and usually near the joint. It rapidly spreads, and involves not only the pastern-bones, but the cartilages of the foot, and spreading around the pasterns and cartilages, thus derives its name. Ringbone is sometimes hereditary; though it is usually occasioned by a strain taken in curvetting, bounding turns, and violent galloping or racing. A coarse or half-bred, fleshy, or bony-legged horse, with short and upright pasterns, is the ordinary subject of this disease.

The Treatment will be similar to spavin. In reality there is no cure, but the lameness may be in a great measure removed by cooling applications, cold water bandage, liniments, and, above all, give the horse rest.

Prof. Spooner says—The best treatment for ringbones after the inflammation has been in great measure removed by cooling applications, is to well rub in the iodine of mercury ointment, washing off the effects on the following day, and thus repeating it again and again. We have by such means succeeded in removing the lameness, diminishing the enlargement, and restoring the animal, in many cases, to a state of usefulness.

FOUNDER, OR ACUTE RHEUMATISM.

This is a very common disease among horses. Founder is produced by driving a horse, when in a state of perspiration, into a pond, exposing him to cold wind or rain, or tying him up in the stable yard while the hostler washes his legs or thighs, and sometimes his body; but excessive exertion alone will, and often does, produce every kind of founder.

SYMPTOMS.—The earliest symptoms of fever in the feet are fidgetyness—frequent shifting of the forelegs. The pulse is quickened, the flanks heaving, the nostrils red, and the horse, by his anxious countenance and—possibly—moaning, indicates great pain. He looks about as if preparing to lie down, he continues to shift his weight from foot to foot, he is afraid to draw his feet sufficiently under him for the purpose of lying down, but at length he drops. His quietness when down will distinguish it from colic or inflammation of the bowels, in both of which the horse is up and down, and frequently rolling and kicking when down. When the grievance is in the feet, the horse experiences so much relief from getting rid of the weight that he is glad to lie as long as he can. He will, likewise, as clearly as in inflammation of the lungs or bowels, point out the seat of disease by looking at the part. His muzzle will often rest on the feet or the affected foot.

The feet will be found hot. The patient will express pain if they are slightly rapped with a hammer, and the artery at the pastern will throb violently. If the disease is suffered to pursue its course, he will be perfectly unable to rise; or, if he is forced to get up, and one foot is lifted, he will stand with difficulty on the others, or perhaps drop at once from intense pain.

TREATMENT.—Youatt says, bleeding is indispensable. If the disease is confined to the fore feet, four quarts of blood should be taken as soon as possible from the toe of each, care being taken to open the artery as well as the vein. The feet may likewise be put into warm water, to quicken the flow of the blood and increase the quantity abstracted. Poultices of linseed meal, made very soft, should cover the whole of the foot and pastern, and be frequently renewed. The shoe should be removed, the sole pared as thin as possible, and the crust, and particularly the quarters, well rasped. This must be done gently, and with a great deal of patience. Sedative and cooling medicines should be diligently administered, consisting of digitalis, nitre, and emetic tartar. About the third day a blister may be tried, taking in the whole of the pastern and the coronet, and washed off the following day, and repeated several times. The horse should be kept on mash diet, unless green meat can be procured, and that should not be given too liberally. Linseed tea, and water acidulated with cream of tartar, form the best drink for patients. When the season will permit, two months' run at grass will be serviceable.

CHRONIC FOUNDER.

The principal difference between this and the acute disease lies in the less activity of the attack and inflammatory fever, and the indefinite duration of the symptoms; the lameness is not persistent, but goes off after exercise, and returns again while the animal is at rest.

The treatment should be similar to that recommended for the acute disease—blood-letting, poultices, fomentations, and blisters, and the last much sooner and much more frequently than in the former disease.

CRAMP.

This is a sudden, involuntary, and painful spasm of a particular muscle. It occasionally attacks the muscles of organic life, but in its most common form only affects the hind extremities, where it is observed by the temporary lameness and stiffness it produces in the hardly worked horse, as he is first led out of the stable in the morning. If any lameness remains, which can be ascertained by pressing the parts, it should be removed by hard rubbing, or by giving the horse a wider or more comfortable stall, if that should appear to be the origin of the difficulty.

SWELLED LEGS.

If it occurs in young horses, and from those that are over-fed and little exercised, sometimes diuretics or purgatives, with proper management will afford relief, if there is a great degree of stiffness and pain—sometimes abscesses appear. Physic or diuretics, or both, must be had recourse to, if not connected with diseases and general debility. Mix cordial with diuretics. Hay bandages, dipped in water, have a good effect for the agricultural horse.

SCRATCHES.

Swelled legs, although distinct from grease, is a disease that is apt to degenerate into it. Scratches is a specific inflammation of the skin and heels, sometimes of the fore feet, but oftener of the hinder ones.

The principal cause of the disease is neglected grooming and care, want of exercise, high feeding, washing the feet and leaving them to dry. The prevention will be proper ventilation, good stabling, grooming, and proper care. It is more likely to affect horses with white feet than others. Some consider the disease contagious.

SYMPTOMS.—The first is heat and tenderness—on applying the hand to the heel and fetlock, the parts will be found hot, and under pressure the animal will evince signs of pain. As the disease progresses, the parts become swolen—infiltrated with serum—thus increasing the inflammatory symptoms, and causing the animal much pain, which he usually evinces by occasionally *catching up the foot.* The hairs stand out horizontally. When the disease attacks both hind legs, the pain is sometimes intense, especially if the horse be plethoric, or his system is charged with morbid humors. In the latter case, the greasy discharge is very profuse; for the pent-up waste matters have now found an outlet, which admit of a free discharge of the fluids of the body.

TREATMENT.—Attention must first be paid to diet, ventilation, and cleanliness. The heels should be gently washed with Castile soap and water, and ointment applied in more advanced cases. Poultice with linseed meal or carrots, boiled and mashed, may be applied, adding a little astringent lotion to renew the irritation and check the discharge. Give the cleansing powder. The following will also be found beneficial, which has been highly recommended, by Prof. Norton and others: Pyroligneous acid, linseed oil, turpentine, of each equal parts. Mix. First wash with water and Castile soap; after wiping them dry, apply the mixture. Repeat night and morning. In order to keep down "proud flesh," the parts may be sprinkled daily with burnt alum. Put on a good coating, cover the sore with dry lint, and apply a bandage over all. Bandages should always be dispensed with if possible.

POULTRY LOUSINESS.

Horses frequently become infected with *lice* from poultry having the roosting place adjoining the stalls. When this is discovered the preventive will be to remove the roosting place, and scald and whitewash the stable.

SYMPTOMS.—The horse is seized with violent itching, shows a disposition to rub and bite himself, strike his belly, is not easy for a moment. At night his torment increases. After this his skin loosens, and his hair and mane sometimes break out with eruptions.

TREATMENT.—In order to destroy the vermin, and, at the same time, to cure the cutaneous eruptions and restore the hair, take linseed oil, 1 ounce; pyroligneous acid, 3 ounces; spirits of turpentine, 1 ounce. Two or three applications of this compound will generally suffice. The parts to which the application has been made must be washed with soap and water. The vermin can also be destroyed by sponging the body with an infusion of lobelia.

HIDE-BOUND.

This term is applied to horses whose coat is *staring*, and skin tight on the ribs, and otherwise out of condition. It is not so much of a disease as a symptom of a disease, particularly of the digestive organs. Every disease that can affect the general system may produce this. Glanders, scratches, chronic cough, farcy founder, are accompanied by hide-bound. Diet too sparing, or want of change in diet, is an unfailing source of it. If the cause is removed, the effect will follow.

TREATMENT.—If no disease appears about the horse, change the diet, clothe the body warmly, give a few mashes and a mild physic, or give alteratives; and there is none better than that which is in common use —pulverized antimony, nitre, and sulphur. Should the horse not feed well, and there is no fever, a slight tonic may be given of ginger. Friction may be used to advantage.

A LIST OF THE

MEDICINES AND RECIPES

USED IN THE

TREATMENT OF THE DISEASES OF THE HORSE.

VINEGAR is a very useful application for sprains and bruises. Equal parts of boiling water and cold vinegar will form a good fomentation.

SPIRIT OF SALT.—This acid is formed by the action of sulphuric acid on common salt. It is decidedly the best liquid caustic we have. For corns, canker, indisposition in the sole to secrete good horn, wounds in the foot not attended by healthy action.

NITRIC ACID.—This is a valuable external application. It is both a caustic and an anti-septic. It destroys fungous excrescences.

SULPHURIC ACID, OR OIL OF VITRIOL.—When mixed with tar, an ounce to the pound, it is a good application for the thrush and canker. A smaller quantity, mixed with olive oil, makes a good stimulating liniment.

ALOES.—There are two kinds used in horse practice, the Barbadoes and the Cape. The Barbadoes aloes have a greater purgative power than the Cape, exclusive of griping less and being safer, and the action of the bowels is kept up longer.

ALUM is used internally in cases of over-purging, in the form of alum whey—two drachms of the powder being added to a pint of hot milk. Its principal use is external. A solution of two drachms to a pint of water, forms alone, or with the addition of a small quantity of white vitriol, a very useful wash for cracked heels, and for grease generally; and also for those forms of swelled legs attended with exudation of moisture through the skin.

ANODYNES.—Opium is the only drug that will lull pain. It may be given as an anodyne, but it will also be an astringent in doses of 1, 2, or 3 drachms.

CAMPHOR.—It diminishes the frequency of the pulse, and softens its tone. When long exhibited, it acts on the kidneys. Externally applied, it is said to be a discutient and an anodyne for chronic sprains, bruises, and tumors.

SPANISH FLIES are the basis of the most approved and useful veterinary blisters. An infusion of 2 ounces of the flies in a pint of oil of turpentine for several days, is occasionally used as a liquid blister; and when sufficiently lowered with common oil, it is called a sweating oil. They have been recommended for the cure of glanders. The dose is from 5 to 8 gr's given daily, but withheld for a day or two when diuresis supervenes.

GUINEA PEPPER.—They are valuable as stimulants. Their beneficial effect in cases of cold has seldom been properly estimated. The dose is from a scruple to half a drachm.

CARAWAY SEEDS.—These and ginger, alone and combined, are the best stimulants used in horse practice.

CASTOR OIL is an expensive medicine. It must be given in large doses.

JAPAN EARTH is a very useful astringent. It is given in over-purging, in doses of 1 or 2 drachms, with opium.

CHARCOAL is occasionally used as an anti-septic, being made into a poultice with linseed meal, and applied to foul and offensive ulcers, and to cracked heels.

VERDIGRIS is usually applied externally as a mild caustic. Either alone, in the form of fine powder, or mixed with an equal quantity of the sugar of lead, it eats down proud flesh, or stimulates old ulcers to healthy action. When boiled with honey and vinegar, it constitutes the farrier's Egyptiacum, certainly of benefit in cankered or ulcerated mouth, and no bad application for thrushes.

BLUE VITRIOL.—It is a favorite tonic with many practitioners. It is principally valuable as an external application, dissolved in water, in the proportion of 2 drachms to a pint; acting as a gentle stimulant. If an ounce is dissolved in the same quantity of water, it becomes a mild caustic. In the former proportion it rouses old ulcers to a healthy action, and disposes even recent wounds to heal more quickly than they otherwise would do; and in the latter it removes fungous granulations or proud flesh. It is also a good application for canker in the foot.

CREOSOTE is much valued on account of its anti-septic properties and in stopping hermorrhages. It is both a stimulant and a tonic. In an undiluted state it acts as a caustic. In the form of a lotion, a liniment, or an ointment, it has been useful in farcy and glanders, also in foot-rot, canker, and thrush. As a caustic, it acts as a powerful stimulant.

DIGITALIS—FOXGLOVE.—The leaves of the common foxglove, gathered about the flowering time, dried carefully in a dark place, and powdered, and kept in a close, black bottle, form one of the most valuable medicines in veterinary practice. It is a direct and powerful sedative, diminishing the frequency of the pulse, and the general irritability of the system, and acting also as a mild diuretic; it is, therefore useful in every inflammatory and febrile complaint, and particularly in inflammation of the chest. It is usually given in combination with emetic tartar and nitre. The average dose is 1 drachm of digitalis, 1½ of emetic tartar, and 3 of nitre, repeated twice or thrice in a day.

DIURETICS constitute a useful class of medicines. They stimulate the kidneys to secrete more than the usual quantity of urine, or to separate a greater than ordinary proportion of the watery parts of the blood.

In swelled legs, cracks, grease, or accumulation of fluid in any part, and in those superficial eruptions and inflammations which are said to be produced by humors floating in the blood, diuretics are evidently beneficial; but they should be as mild as possible, and not oftener given or continued longer than the case requires.

GENTIAN stands at the head of the vegetable tonics, and is a stomachic as well as a tonic. 4 drachms of gentian, 2 of camomile, 1 of carbonate of iron, and 1 of ginger, will make an excellent tonic ball. An infusion of gentian is one of the best applications to putrid ulcers.

GINGER is as valuable as a cordial as gentian is as a tonic. It is the basis of the cordial ball, and it indispensable in the tonic ball.

HELEBORE (BLACK).—This is used mostly as a local application, and as such it is a very powerful stimulant.

INJECTIONS.—See clysters.

IODINE.—This is one of the most valuable drugs used in the veterinary practice. It is used in reducing every species of tumors. It is used in various forms. Iodine of potassium is best administered internally, as a promoter of absorption. Combined with the sulphate of copper, it forms a powerful and useful tonic; whilst in the form of iodine of mercury, and combined with lard or palm oil, it becomes a powerful blister, and a useful promoter of absorption.

CHLORIDE OF LIME is exceedingly valuable. Diluted with twenty times its quantity of water, it helps to form the poultice applied to offensive discharges. The fœtid smell of fistulous withers, poll-evil, canker, and ill-conditioned wounds, is immediately removed, and the ulcers are more disposed to heal.

LINSEED is often used instead of water for the drink of the horse with sore throat or cartarrh, or disease of the urinary organs, or of the bowels.

MASHES constitute a very important part of horse provender, whether in sickness or health.

MUSTARD SINAPIS.—This will be found useful if, in inflammation of the chest or bowels, it is well rubbed on the chest or abdomen.

NITROUS ETHER (SPIRIT OF) is a very useful medicine in the advanced stages of fever.

OPIUM, however under-rated by some, is a valuable drug; but it is a powerful anti-spasmodic, sedative, and astringent.

PALM OIL is the very best substance that can be used for making masses and balls.

PITCH.—The best plaster for sand-crack consists of 1 pound of pitch and an ounce of yellow beeswax melted together.

NITRATE OF POTASH (NITRE) is a valuable cooling medicine and a mild diuretic, and, therefore, it should enter into the composition of every fever ball. Dose is from 2 to 4 drachms.

POULTICES.—Few horsemen are aware of the value of these simple applications in abating inflammation, relieving pain, cleansing wounds, and disposing them to heal. Linseed meal forms the best general poultice, because it longest retains the moisture.

SEDATIVES are medicines that subdue irritation, repress spasmodic action, or deaden pain. Digitalis, hellebore, opium, turpentine, are medicines of this kind.

SUGAR OF LEAD.—See under lead.

SULPHUR.—It is an excellent alterative, combined usually with antimony and nitre, and particularly for mange, surfeit, grease, hide-bound, or want of condition; and it is a useful ingredient in the cough and fever ball.

TAR, melted with an equal quantity of grease, forms a good stopping of the farrier. But its principal virtue seem to consist in preventing the penetration of dirt and water to the wounded part; and it is used with the usual cough medicine, and in doses of 2 or 3 drachms for chronic cough.

TURPENTINE is one of the best diuretics, in doses of half an ounce, and made into a ball with linseed meal and powdered ginger. The oil of turpentine is an excellent anti-spasmodic. For the removal of colic it stands unrivalled.

ZINC (CALAMINE POWDER).—Five parts of lard and one of resin are melted together, and when these begin to get cool, two parts of the calamine, reduced to an impalpable powder, are stirred in. If the wound is not healthy, a small quantity of common turpentine may be added. This salve justly deserves the name which it has gained—"The Healing Ointment." The calamine is sometimes sprinkled with advantage on cracked heels and superficial sores.

RECEIPTS.

WONDERFUL LINIMENT.—Two ounces oil of spike, 2 do. origanum, 2 do. hemlock, 2 do. wormwood, 4 do. sweet oil, 2 do. spts. ammonia, 2 do. gum camphor, 2 do. spts. turpentine, and 1 quart of proof spirits 95 per cent. Mix well together, and bottle tight.

For sprains, bruises, lameness, &c., &c., the above liniment cannot be equalled, and is actually worth $100 to any person keeping valuable horses. Omit the turpentine, and you have the best liniment ever made for human ails, such as rheumatism, sprains, &c. Whenever an outward application is required, try it, and prove its virtues. It acts like magic.

RHEUMATIC LINIMENT.—Take alcohol, ½ pint; oil of origanum, ½ oz.; cayenne, ½ oz.; gum myrrh, ½ oz.; 1 tea-spoonful of lobelia, and let it stand one day, then bathe the part affected. We paid $5 for this recipe.

RELIEF LINIMENT.—Take ½ pint linseed oil, add ½ pint spts. turpentine, 1 oz. origanum, and 1 oz. oil of vitriol; an excellent liniment for rheumatism, sprains, bruises, &c. Try, and prove it.

CHLOROFORM LINIMENT.—For relieving suffering in case of burns, &c. Mix chloroform and cod-liver oil.

SOAP LINIMENT.—Take 1 oz. origanum, 1 oz. Castile soap, 1 pint alcohol. For swellings, &c.

GENERAL LINIMENT.—Turpentine, one half-pint; linseed oil, one half-pint; aquamonia, 4 oz.; tr. of iodine, 1. Shake it all well. This is used for different things spoken of in the different receipts, sores or swellings, sprains, &c.

BLACK LINIMENT.—This is good to apply on poll-evil—fistula. Take of linseed oil, ½ pint; tr. of iodine, 8 oz.; turpentine, 4 oz.; oil of origanum, 1 oz. Shake all well, and apply it every day. Rub it in well with your hand. Wash the part clean with soap and water before applying it. This is good on any swelling.

JOHNSTON'S LINIMENT.—Take oil of origanum, 1 oz.; alcohol, one half pint; oil of cedar, one half ounce; oil of cloves, one half ounce; turpentine, one half ounce; olive oil, 8 ounces. Shake all well. This is used for almost all complaints of the muscles.

OPODELDOC.—Take alcohol, half a gallon; 2 pounds of Castile soap, 4 oz. gum camphor, 2 oz. oil of amber; place the alcohol into a pot in hot water, shave up the soap, and keep it hot until all disolves, and you have the old original opodeldoc.

GREEN OINTMENT.—Take 6 lbs. lard, put into ten-gallon kettle, add 2 gallons of water, cut jimpson-weeds and fill them in and cook them four to six hours, slow, and cook all the water out, then put into jars. Add to each pound of ointment 1 ounce of turpentine. This is a good and cheap stable ointment—good for galls, cuts, scratches, &c.

SLOAN'S OINTMENT.—Take mutton tallow, 4 lbs.; beeswax, one half-pound; resin, one half-pound; turpentine, 8 oz. Melt over a slow fire, and, when partly cold, add the turpentine, and you have the same ointment. Sloan sells to cure everything; try it, and prove its value.

IODINE OINTMENT.—Get 1 oz. of the grease iodine, 1 pint of alcohol. Let this stand in the sun two days, and this is the tincture of iodine. Take 2 oz. of tincture and one half-pint of lard, mix well, and you have the iodine ointment. This is used wherever the receipts refer to the ointment.

WHITE OINTMENT.—For rheumatism, sprains, burns, swellings, bruises, or any inflammation on man or beast, chapped hands or lips, black eyes, or any kind of bruise. Take fresh butter, 2 lbs.; tr. of iodine, half ounce; oil of origanum, 2 oz. Mix this well for fifteen minutes, and it is fit for use. Apply it every night. Rub it in well with your hand. If for human flesh, lay on warm flannel.

BLUE OINTMENT.—Take the ointment of resin, 4 oz.; half oz. of finely-ground verdigris, 2 oz. turpentine, 2 lbs. mutton tallow, half oz. oil of origanum, half oz. tr. of iodine. Mix all well. This is one of the best medicines that can be made for scratches, hoof-evil, cuts, and is good to apply on fistula after the rowels have been taken out.

HOOF OINTMENT.—Take resin, 4 oz.; beeswax, 6 oz.; lard, 2 lbs. Melt together. Pour it into a pot, and 3 oz. of turpentine, 2 oz. of finely-powdered verdigris, 1 lb. tallow. Stir all until it gets cool. This is one of the best medicines for the hoof ever used. It is good for corks or bruises of the feet.

HOOF LIQUID.—For tender feet, hoof-bound, &c. Linseed or neatsfoot oil, half a pint of either; turpentine, 4 oz.; oil of tar, 6 oz.; origanum, 2 oz. Shake this well and apply it as the directions for the ointment. This is the best, if the horse has been lame long; it penetrates the hoof sooner than the ointment. Both of them should be applied at night.

HOOF-EVIL OR THRUSH, GREASE HEELS.—Bleed, and physic, and poultice the foot with boiled turnips and some fine-ground charcoal. This must be done at night, for two or three nights; then wash the foot clean with Castile soap and soft water, and apply the blue ointment every day. Keep the horse on a floor, and he will be well in twelve days.

HOOF-BOUND, OR TENDER FEET.—Never have the feet spread at the heels nor rasped above the nail holes, for it will do the foot an injury. Follow the directions given here. Use either the hoof ointment or the hoof liquid. Apply it according to directions. For hoof-bound or tender feet, apply it all around the top of the hoof down one inch every third day. If for split hoof apply it every day. First, have a stiff shoe on the foot and cleanse the cut or crack. Never cut or burn for it.

HOOF AIL.—Apply blue vitriol, and put on a tarred rag to keep out the dirt.

No. 2. Wash well with warm soap-suds, wipe dry with a cloth; then take 2 spoonsful of common table salt, 2 spoonsful of copperas, pulverize; 4 spoonsful of soft soap. Mix well. Spread it upon a thick cloth, apply to the foot, then confine it with a bandage. Let it remain 12 hours, then wash as before.

HOOF-BOUND.—Pare the heel of the hoof till it is as flat and natural as a colt's, then take equal parts pitch pine and butter simmered together and anoint the heel.

HEAVES.—Take 1 lb. of resin, 1 lb. of saltpetre, 8 oz. alum, 1 oz. of assafœtida; 4 oz. of sulphur. Pulverize and mix. Give 1 tea-spoonful once a day in his feed. This is also a good medicine for putting a horse in condition.

PREPARATION FOR GELDING HORSES.—Take 2 oz. corrosive sublimate, 1 oz. gum kino, 1 oz. red precipitate.

SPRAIN IN THE STIFLE.—Symptoms—The horse holds up his foot, moans when moved, swells in the stifle. This is what is called stifling. There is no such thing as this joint getting out of place. Cure—Bleed 2 gallons, foment the stifle with hot water, rub it dry, then bathe it well with the general liniment every morning and night. Give him a mash and he will be well. Never allow any stifle-shoe or cord on the foot or leg.

HOW TO CURE CORNS.—Take off the shoe, cut out the corns, and drop in a few drops of muriatic acid, then make the shoes so as they will not bear on the part affected. Apply the hoof liquid to the hoof to remove the fever. This is a sure treatment. We never knew it to fail.

CORNS.—Take the shoe off and give the horse a free run at grass for a few weeks. This will frequently cure.

FOUNDER IN THE FIRST STAGES —Bleed from the neck-vein 2 or 3 gallons or until he falls, then give the following: Half oz. of aloes, 4 drachms of gamboge, half oz. oil of sassafras. Make this into a pill, give it, and give him all the sassafras tea he will drink; turn up his feet, and fill them full of boiling hot lard; bathe his legs in hot water, and rub them well. This will never fail to cure in 48 hours.

No. 2. Physic and poultice the feet.

No. 3. Mix 1 pint of sunflower seed in his food.

SPAVIN OR RING-BONE.—Take 1 pint spts. turpentine, 1 pint of oil spike, 4 oz. saltpetre, 4 oz. of alum, 2 oz. oil vitriol. Bathe the part affected thoroughly every other day for one week, and if this does not effect a cure continue it longer. This has cured spavins of nine years' standing. This receipt has been used with great success.

SPAVIN AND RING-BONE MEDICINE.—Take of cantharides, 2 oz.; mercurial ointment, 4 oz.; tr. of iodine, 8 oz.; turpentine, 4 oz.; corrosive sublimate, 3 drachms. Mix all well with 2 lbs. of lard. Color it if you like. Follow the directions here given.

If for ring-bone or bone-spavin, cut off the hair from the part affected, and merely grease the lump with the ointment. Rub it in well with the naked hand. In two days grease the part with lard, and in four days wash it off with soap and water, and apply the ointment again. So repeat it every four days. If for wind-galls, or bog-spavin, or curb, apply the ointment every six days. This recipe has been sold for $300.

SPAVIN.—Camphor dissolved in spirits of turpentine, applied until the hair starts.

No. 2. Oil vitriol, origanum, cedar oil, Spanish flies, equal parts; 8 oz. turpentine.

To Cure Ring-Bone when First Coming.—Dissolve one quarter-pound of salt-petre in one quart soft water, and wash with it twice a day. This will stop the growth and lameness, and not remove the hair.

Ring-Bone.—Take of spts. turpentine, oil of spike, of each 1 oz.; bottle and mix well; then add 1 oz. of oil vitriol. Bathe the diseased part well for three days, and drive it in by the application of a hot iron; then suspend it for three days to prevent the part becoming too sore, then apply the remedy again. The sore should be treated with lard or ointment. This will cure the disease if not of too long standing.

Poll Evil.—Cure before it breaks. Run a rowel or seton from the lower part of the swelling to the top, through the centre of the enlargement, then make the following lotion: Take of salamoniac, 2 oz.; and turpentine spirits, half pint; 4 oz. linseed oil, and 4 oz. spts. tar. Shake all well, and apply it all over the swelling every other day. Let the seton stay in until all the swelling is gone down; move it every day, and when all is gone draw it out. Bleed when you first open it. Keep the part clean.

Poll Evil after it Breaks.—If you find by probing it that the pipes run down towards the surface, run down a seton through the bottom of the pipe, and anoint it with the following ointment: Take of mercurial ointment, 4 oz.; and of cantharides, half an ounce. Anoint the seton every day until it runs a bloody matter, then draw it out, if the pipes run down to the centre of the shoulders; then run down a piece of the nitre of silver to the bottom, and use the liquid in the next following receipt. Apply it on the sore every day. Keep the part clean with soap and water.

Liquid for Poll Evil.—Take olive oil, 6 ounces; turpentine, half oz.; oil of origanum, half oz.; American or seneka oil, 8 oz. Mix well, and apply it to the part affected, after the nitre of silver has been used. Apply this every few days until it heals up. The cleaner you keep the part the better.

Poll Evil and Fistula.—Clean the sore throughout with soap-suds, sound the pipe or pipes, find their direction and depth, then take stiff paper, roll it in a horn shape about the size of a goose-quill, fill with arsenic or potash, double over the ends, insert the pipe, and push or drive it to the bottom. Serve all the pipes in the same manner. It will break loose in three to six weeks. Cleanse it one day with soap-suds, and next with a wash composed of 1 tea-spoonful of white vitriol, and 1 do. burnt copperas, 1 do. burnt alum, 1 of gunpowder, in one pint of rain water. Oil the sore well after washing.

FISTULA.—Take 1 pint of alcohol, half pint turpentine, 1 oz. indigo. Apply once a day.

TO DRIVE OFF POLL EVIL BEFORE IT BREAKS.—Take 4 oz. oil of spike, 1 of British oil, one-eighth of white vitriol, 1 of extract of mullen hearts. Apply twice a day. Shake well before you apply. Give the cleansing powder to cleanse the blood.

THRUSH OR SPAVIN.—Take 2 oz. oil of St, John, 1 oz. of oil of vitriol, 1 oz. oil turpentine, 3 oz. of whiskey. For spavin or ring-bone add 2 oz. of mercurial ointment. This is a valuable receipt.

CONDITION POWDERS.—Take 2 lbs. of resin, 1 lb. ginger, 1 lb. cassar, ½ lb. saltpetre. Pulverize fine and mix together. Give 1 table-spoonful every other day.

WATER FARCY.—This is a swelling along under the chest, and forward to the breast. Bleed, rowel in the breast and all along the swelling, six inches apart. Apply the general liniment to the swelling. Move the rowels every day. Let them stay in until the swelling goes down. Give soft food—mashes—with the cleansing powder in it. This is dropsy.

TOO FREE DISCHARGE OF URINE.—Give one half oz. of the tr. of cantharides every morning for ten or twelve days, and if not entirely well, repeat it again, and bleed one gallon from the neck—give clean food. The cause is rotten or musty grain, or too free use of turpentine. Keep him open with mashes and green food.

DISEASE OF THE LIVER, OR YELLOW WATER.—Give the following ball every morning until it operates upon the bowels. Take 7 drachms of aloes, and 1 drachm of calomel, 4 drachms of ginger, and molasses enough to make it into a ball, wrap it in paper and give it; give scalded bran and oats, grass if it can be got; when his bowels have moved, stop the physic, and give 1 oz. spirits of camphor in a half pint of water every morning for twelve days; rowel in the breast, and give a few doses of cleansing powder. Turn him out.

FRESH WOUNDS.—First, stop the wound by tying the arteries, or by applying the following wash: 4 gr. of nitre of silver, 1 oz. of soft water. Wet the wound with this and then draw the edges together by stitches one inch apart, then wash clean, and if any swelling in twenty-four hours, bleed, and apply the blue ointment, or any of the liniments spoken of. Keep the bowels open.

BRUISES.—Take Arnica blossoms steeped in whiskey.

CURE FOR BILES ON HORSES —Permit the patient to have a run for 5 or 6 weeks in a good pasture, and give a little physic in shorts or meal.

CURE FOR CRAMP.—Give a dose of cathartic medicines and hot fomentations to the limbs, and a little rest.

BALLS FOR WORMS.—Barbadoes Aloes 6 dra., powdered ginger 1½ oz. oil of wormwood 20 drops, powdered natron, 2 dra.; molasses to form a ball.

BALL FOR HIDE BOUND.—Barbadoes Aloes, 1 oz, Castile soap, 9 dra., ginger 6 dra.

PHYSIC-BALL.—One half ounce of aloes, 8 drachms of gamboge, 20 drops of the oil of juniper; make it into a pill with a few drops of molasses; wrap it up in thin paper and grease it; draw out the tongue with the left hand; place the gag in the mouth, run the pill back with the right hand until it drops off, then let the head down and give a sup of water. First, prepare the horse by giving one or two mashes.

LIQUID BLISTERER.—Take alcohol, 1 pint; turpentine, one half pint; aquamonia, 4 oz.; oil of origanum 1 oz.; apply this as spoken of every three hours until it blisters. Do not repeat oftener than once in eight days, or seven at least, or it will kill the hair.

HEALING OINTMENT.—Take five parts of lard, one of rosin, melt together; when they begin to get cool add two parts of calomine powder. If the wound is unhealthy add a little turpentine.

GALLS ON HORSES.—Bath the parts affected with spirits saturated with alum.

GRUBS IN HORSES.—Take a teaspoonful of red precipitate, form into a ball, repeat, if necessary, in 30 minutes.

WORMS.—Give one quart of strong tea made of worm-wood at night, the next day give 7 drachms of aloes, 2 drachms of calomel, make it into a ball and give it; give no cold water for 48 hours; make it milk-warm; give him 2 or 8 bran mashes, and some of the cleansing-powder; if he shows any more symptoms, repeat the dose in three weeks. This will never fail.

WARTS.—Cut them out by the roots—take the tenakulum or hook, run it through the warts, and draw and cut round it, and draw it out; if it should bleed too much, take 5 grains of nitre of silver, and 1 oz. of water; wet a sponge, and merely touch the part with this wash, and it will stop them; treat it as any fresh wound—still, every time you wash it, scratch

K

the scab off, so the scar will be small. This is the only sure way to treat them.

GROGGY KNEES.—This can be cured in the first stages, but if of long standing, there is no cure Have shoes made thick at the toe and thin at the heels; take linseed oil, half pint; alcohol, 4 oz.: 1 oz. camphor spirits; 2 oz. laudanum—shake and apply to back part of legs, rub it in well every 4 days; still increase the thickness of the shoes at the toe.

SORE MOUTH OR TONGUE.—Take of borax 3 drachms, and 2 drachms of sugar of lead, half oz. of alum, one pint of sage tea—shake all well together, and wash the mouth out every morning. Give no hay for twelve days.

CLEANSING POWDER.—This is to be used when the blood is out of order —good to restore lost appetite—yellow water; and wherever it is to be used, it is spoken of. Take 1 pound of good ginger; 4 oz. powdered gentian; 1 oz. nitre; half oz. crude antimony—mix all well. Give one large spoonful every day, in wet food. This is perfectly safe.

SICK STOMACH.—Bleed half a gallon, then if he will eat a mash give him one; give no hay; then give him half oz. rhubarb every night until it moves his bowels; then take of gentian root, 4 oz.; fenugreek, 2 oz.; nitre, one-half oz.—mix and give a large spoonful every day, do not give him too much to eat when his appetite returns.

HORSE POWDER.—For distemper, hidebound, farcy, colts, and all lingering diseases which arise from impurity of the blood or lungs. Take 1 lb. comfrey root, ¼ lb. antimony, ¼ lb. sulphur, 3 oz. saltpetre, ¼ lb. laurel berries, ¼ lb. juniper berries, ¼ lb. anise-seed, ¼ lb. rosin, 3 oz. alum, 5 oz. copperas, ¼ lb. masterworth, ¼ lb. gum powder. Mix to a powder, and give one teaspoonful in his food once a day, till cured; keep the horse dry, and from water for six hours after using it.

TONIC DRENCH.—For weakness and debility. Take port wine, 3 oz. tincture of cinnamon, ¼ oz. powdered goldenseal 4 drachms.

LUNG FEVER.—Bleed four gallons from the neck vein, and take one oz. of aconite, add to it half gallon of cold water; drench him with one gill of it every 3 hours, blister him over the lungs, then give him water to drink that hay has been boiled in, and to each gallon of it one oz. of gum arabic, and half an ounce of spirits of nitre—give this every four hours, rub well, foment and rub the legs with alcohol and camphor, until they get warm—do not move him. Keep him in an open stall, if hot weather.

EYE LOTION.—Take of linseed oil one pint, add to it two oz. of spirits of ether, gum camphor half an oz. Let it stand in some warm place until the oil cuts the gum, and it is fit for use.

STING OF BEES.—Take olive oil, and lime water, equal parts. Apply it externally.

EYE-WASH.—Take of sugar of lead 2 drachms, white vitriol 1 drachm, add to this 1 quart of soft water; let it stand for 6 or 9 hours, and it is fit for use. Wash the eyes out well every morning, after first washing the eyes out well with cold water; fol'ow this up for 8 or 4 weeks, and then if the eyes are not much better, bleed and give a mild physic. The horse should be kept on low diet, and not over heated or worked too hard; scalded shorts and oats are good.

MANGE AND SURFEIT.—Bleed and physic, then take sulphur one-half pound, 2 pounds lard; mix well, grease the part affected every three or four days, stand the horse in the sun until all dries in, give him a few doses of the cleansing-powder.

CONTRACTION OF THE NECK.—If it is taken in the first stages, bleed from the neck two gallons, then ferment or bathe the part well with hot water, rub it dry and take the general liniment and apply it every day, two or three times; this will cure. If it is of long standing, then blister all along the part affected, with the liquid blister. Do this every three weeks until he is well, and rub with the white ointment.

DROPS TO MAKE OLD HORSES YOUNG.—Take the tr. of asafœtida 1 oz.; tr. of cantharides, 1 oz.; oil of cloves, 1 oz.; oil of cinnamon, 1 oz.; antimony, 2 oz.; fenugreek, one oz.; fourth proof brandy, half gallon; let it stand ten or twelve days, and give ten drops in a pail of water—or one gallon.

AN EDITOR'S TROTTERS.

Robert Bonner's Stables. His latest purchases. Gossip about Famous Roadsters.

There is a widespread passion in America for the ownership of trotting horses, and in this respect Mr. Bonner, the editor of the *New York Ledger*, is unusually fortunate. The perfection of his stables is a matter of national comment, for, with beauty of architecture, they combine every requisite for the health and comfort of the horses. The ventilation and drainage are excellent. Every stall has a false floor, through which all refuse passes to a sub-floor of cement, whence it is carried into the sewers. The floor on which the horse stands is perfectly level, thus avoiding that straining of the tendons of the legs consequent upon the standing on an inclined surface. The sides of the boxes are of smooth wooden panels, which present no hold for the horse to seize with his teeth, and thus prevents his acquiring the habits of biting and "cribbing." The partitions are carried high enough to prevent the horses from annoying each other; the doors are of ornamental iron work, and around the building, outside, is a tan-bark walk for exercising the horses in bad weather. Every appliance that could possibly reduce labor and improve the condition of the horses has been adopted.

The first horse the visitor inquires for is Dexter, undoubtedly the highest type of the American trotter. He is a brown horse, with white legs, stands 15¼ hands high, and is 18 years old. His head and neck are finely formed, his eyes brilliant, his shoulders well placed, his legs and feet arm, and his back and loins powerful. For a horse of his size, his thighs are immense. It is almost unnecessary to allude to his breeding. He can be traced to imported Messenger on the sire's side, and to imported Diomed (the winner of the first English Derby) on the dam's side. He was first trained by Hiram Woodruff, and it is not a little singular that in Mr. Bonner's stable, standing in adjoining stalls, are the two horses (Dexter and Peerless) behind which Hiram Woodruff made the best time he ever made in his life, driving the former in harness and the latter to wagon, in 2:23¼. But Woodruff died before Dexter's speed was fully developed, though he had a premonition that even the 2:18 1-5 which he had seen him make under the saddle on the Fashion Course would in time be surpassed. He was right in this expectation, for 10,000 people saw Dexter trot a heat against Ethan Allen and his running mate in 2:16, although by an unjust regulation, the horse was not allowed to claim that record. It is not asserted, however, that he is entitled to the record of 2:16 as a winning record, but that it is justly his due as the time record of a public performance.

Budd Doble has stated that he drove him in 2:14¾ in private, while in a public race he drove him in 2:17¼, and a half mile in 1:06. Good judges believe that by far his greatest achievement was the day when Mr. Bonner drove him on the Prospect Park Course, wagon and driver weighing 319½ pounds, in 2:21¼—a performance which, considering the weight carried and the state of the track, was equal to 2:14. It is now four years since Mr. Bonner gave his check for 33,000 for Dexter, and withdrew the horse from the turf, and there is little doubt that Dexter's speed is greater now than it was when he trotted in 2:17¼ in Buffalo in the hands of Budd Doble. When Mr. Bonner purchased him it was said that he would be valueless, as he could not be driven with safety on the road. But kindness and good management produced their legitimate results, and Mr. Bonner drives him regularly on the road and through Central Park.

In the next stall stands the gray mare Peerless, a daughter of American Star and a Messenger mare. Like Dexter, she was bred in that nursery for fast horses, Orange County, and like him also was educated by Hiram Woodruff, who drove her in public a mile to wagon in 2:23¼—a performance which only Dexter has surpassed. Peerless has proved a failure as a brood mare, but is a favorite roadster with Mr. Bonner, who often drives her double with the veteran Lantern, the two making a fine and fast team.

Lantern comes next, and it is only the curve of the back that shows his age, for his eye is as bright and his legs as clean as on the day he trotted his famous double-team match against Ethan Allen and mate, 14 years ago. Although 24 years old, he is still fast, and makes an excellent companion for Peerless, few being able to pass them on the road. In the next stall stands the California mare Princess, the once famous opponent of Flora Temple. She was purchased as a brood mare, to be mated with Edward Everett, the sire of Joe Elliott, Judge Fullerton, and Startle, and has long been quite lame, but it is anticipated that she will soon recover From her union with Hambletonian sprang Happy Medium.

The stout black colt in the adjoining box is Mambrino Bertie, Mr. Bonner's latest purchase. Bred by Dr. Herr, of Lexington, Ky.; this colt astonished everybody by trotting a mile, last Fall, when a two-year old, over the Cincinnati Course, in 2:41, and repeating, half an hour afterward, in 2:43½. He has since trotted in 2:36½; but not being thoroughly acclimated, Mr. Bonner does not purpose hurrying him. He is a handsome colt, wonderfully developed for a three-year old, and will assuredly make a fast trotter in time. The bay horse in the next box ranks highest in Mr. Bonner's esteem. This is the four-year old colt Startle, by Edward Everett, which was purchased from George Alley, last Fall, for $20,000, immediately after winning the Three-year-old Stakes, distancing his opponent, Lothair, in the fast time of 2:36½. Startle has massive, muscular quarters, indicating the possession of immense powers. Perhaps no colt ever made such rapid progress in trotting speed as this horse, for when Carl Burr purchased him, in June last year, he could not beat 3:20, and in the following September he won his first race in 2:36½. Last month Mr. Bonner drove him a mile on the Fleetwood Park Course, on a slow track, in 2:23, and, had the day and course been favorable, he could have reduced the time considerably. As Startle is only four years old, he has plenty of time for maturing and improving, and experienced judges believe that, when Dexter's time of 2:16 is surpassed, Startle is the horse destined to do it.

The bay gelding Joe Elliott next shown, trotted a heat over the Seacaucus Course, N. J., in 1869, in 2:34, his name then being Boyant Colt. Mr. Bonner paid $10,000 for him, and placed him with Carl Burr for training. A few months ago he made a mile on the Fleetwood Course in 2:18½. Bruno occupies the next box, and never was in more superb condition than now. Since Mr. Bonner bought him of Mr. Phyfe he has greatly improved in speed. As a four-year-old he made the best record in a public race, trotting a mile in 2:30 in a gale of wind. With his sister, Brunette, he made also the fastest double-team time, having trotted a mile in 2:25½. Last on the list stands Pocahontas, the beautiful daughter of the famous pacing mare of the same name and Ethan Allen. A mare of more perfect symmetry and beauty was never foaled; her action when in motion is the perfection of trotting, combining ease, elegance, power and speed, in an extraordinary degree. She has trotted only one race in public, namely, against Blackstone Belle, at Boston, which she won easily. It is said an amount, even larger than that paid for Dexter, was paid for her. That Mr. Bonner in purchasing her was not mistaken, appears from the fact that she has since trotted a mile under saddle, ridden by John Murphy, in 2:19½. She is an excellent team mare, and there need not be much surprise if next season she and Buruo make the best time ever made by a double team.

2.30 HORSES.

BY AJAX.

Goldsmith Maid, by Alexander's Abdallah, dam by Abdallah... 2:17
Dexter, by Hambletonian, dam by American Star.............. 2:17 1-4
Lady Thorne, by Mambrino Chief, dam by Gano, by American
    Eclipse.. 2:18 1-4
American Girl, by Amos' Clay, dam said to be thoroughbred... 2:19
George Palmer, by the Bogus horse, dam a Clay mare.......... 2:19 1-4
Flora Temple, by One-Eyed Hunter............................ 2:19 3-4
Henry, by Magna Charta 2:20 1-4
Mountain Boy, by Edward Everett, dam by Roebuck............. 2:20 1-2
General Butler, by Smith Burr, by Napoleon.................. 2:21
Rolla Golddust, by Golddust, to saddle...................... 2:21
George Wilkes, by Hambletonian.............................. 2:22
Princess, by Michael Reaker................................. 2:22
Jay Gould, by Hambletonian, dam by American Star............ 2:22
Rockingham, to saddle....................................... 2:22 1-4
Lucy, by G. M. Patchen, dam May Day......................... 2:22 1-2
G. M. Patchen, by C. M. Clay, dam by Trustee................ 2:22 1-2
Fearnaught, by Young Morrill................................ 2:23 1-4
Bashaw, Jr., by Green's Bashaw.............................. 2:23 1-2
Rhode Island, by Whitehall, by North American............... 2:23 1-2
Hotspur, by Ethan Allen, dam by Abdallah.................... 2:23 1-2
Billy Barr, (formerly W. B. Whiteman,) by Ethan Allen....... 2:23 3-4
Kirkwood, by Green's Bashaw................................. 2:24
Draco Prince, by Draco, dam Vermont Black Hawk.............. 2:24
Ch. Medoc, (formerly John Morgan,) by Pilot, dam by Medoc... 2:24

Beppo, by Hambletonian, dam by Abdallah.... .... 2:24 1-2
Chicago, (formerly Rocky,) by Ole Bull, by Pilot, dam by American Eclipse... 2:24
Toronto Chief, by Royal George........................ 2:24 1-4
Major Allen, (formerly Locust,) by Young Ethan Allen.......... 2:24 1-4
California Damsel, by son of Long Island Black Hawk......... 2:24 1-2
Prince Hartford, by Nonpareil, son of Long Island Black Hawk 2:24 1-2
Pilot Temple, by Pilot, Jr., dam Flora Temple's dam.......... 2:24 1-2
Myron Perry, by Young Columbus, dam by Hopkins' Abdallah.. 2:24 1-2
Green Mountain Maid, by Harris' Hambletonian............... 2:24 3-4
Silas Rich, by Young Priam...................................... 2:24 3-4
Clara G., to saddle.............................. 2:25
G. M. Patchen, Jr., (California Patchen,) by G. M. Patchen, dam Bellfounder mare......................... 2:25
W. H. Allen, by Volunteer, dam by Abdallah.................... 2:25
Mac... 2:25
Commordore Vanderbilt, by Young Columbus................ 2:25
Frank Vernon, (formerly Panic,) by Sherman's Black Hawk (North Horse,) dam Vermont Hambletonian............... 2:25
Ethan Allen, by Hill's Black Hawk........................... 2:25
Yellow Jacket....................................... 2:25
Lancet, by Vermont Black Hawk, to saddle.................... 2:25
Brown Dick, by 2d Star.. 2:25 1-4
Gray Eagle. (thoroughbred,) by Gray Eagle, dam by imp. Trustee.................................. 2:25 1-2
Fannie Allen, by Ethan Allen, dam Cherub, by Abdallah....... 2:25 1-2
Gray Mack, by son of Hill's Black Hawk...................... 2:25 1-2
Centreville, by Henry Clay................................... 2:25 1-2
Tecony, by Sportsman............................. 2:25 1-2
Nonesuch, by Daniel Lambert, by Ethan Allen, dam by son of Vermont Black Hawk...................... 2:25 1-2
Judge Fullerton, by Edward Everett...................... 2:25 1-4
Tom Jefferson, by Toronto Chief, dam by Wagner.............. 2:25 1-2
Charles E. Loew, by G. M. Patchen, dam by Abdallah.......... 2:25 1-2
J. J. Bradley...................................... 2:25 1-2
Byron, by Field's Royal George, dam by Morgan............... 2:25 1-2
Harry Harley, (formerly Columbia Chief,) by Young Columbus, dam by Harris' Hambletonian............................. 2:25 3-4
Jeff Davis.................................... 2:25 3-4
Colonel Russell................................ 2:25 3-4
License...................................... 2:25 3-4

Belle Strickland, by Eaton Horse............................... 2:26
Billy Haskins, by Ed Forest, dam Pilot, Jr...................... 2:26
Belle of Portland... 2:26
Tattler, by Pilot, Jr., dam by Medoc............................ 2:26
Tackey, by Pilot, Jr.. 2:26
W. K. Thomas, by Osceola, by son of Pilot...................... 2:26
May Queen, by May Day.. 2:26
Confidence... 2:26
Huntress, by Volunteer, dam by American Star................... 2:26
Triumph, (formerly Joe).. 2:25 1-4
Ben Cumming, by Columbus, dam Mambrino......................... 2:26
H. W. Genet, by son of G. M. Patchen........................... 2:26
Lady Suffolk, by Engineer...................................... 2:26
Surprise, by Harry Clay.. 2:26
Cooly, by Daniel Boone (a pacer)............................... 2:26
Leviathan, to saddle... 2:26
Sleepy John.. 2:26 1-4
Bay Whalebone.. 2:26 1-4
Lady Emma, by Jupiter, dam by Abdallah......................... 2:26 1-4
Royal John, by Woodstock Morrill............................... 2:26 1-4
Queen of the West, by Pilot, Jr................................ 2:26 1-4
Stockbridge Chief.. 2:26 1-2
Black Mack... 2:26 1-2
Matthew Smith.. 2:26 1-2
Mohawk, Jr., by Mohawk, by Long Island Black Hawk.............. 2:26 1-2
Susie, by Hampden Boy, grandsire Vermont Black Hawk............ 2:26 1-2
Little Fred, dam Dirigo, by Drew............................... 2:26 3-4
Pocahontas, by Ethan Allen, dam Pocahontas, the pacer.......... 2:26 3-4
Sea Foam, by Young Columbus.................................... 2:26 3-4
Gilbraith Knox, by General Knox, he by North Horse............. 2:26 3-4
Clara, (late Crazy Jane,) by Sager Horse....................... 2:27
Idol, by Black Warrior... 2:27
Highland Maid, by Saltram...................................... 2:27
Western Girl, (formerly Angeline,) by son of Bellfounder....... 2:27
Look Out... 2:27
Sir Walter... 2:27
Lottery, by Hambletonian....................................... 2:27
Aggy Down, to saddle... 2:27
General Taylor, to saddle...................................... 2:27
Sorrel Dan, by Magna Charta.................................... 2:27

Lady Woodruff, by Washington.................................... 2:27
Tammany, by son of Rising Sun.................................. 2:27
Ben Higdon, by Abdallah....................................... 2:27
Uncle Abe, by Young Morrill................................... 2:27
Tennessee, by Commodore, dam by Hill's Black Hawk........... 2:27
Prince, ch., by Jupiter Abdallah, dam by Trustee............. 2:27
Lady Mac, to saddle (Hambletonian)........................... 2:27
North Star Mambrino, by Mambrino Chief. 2:27 1-4
Star of the West.. 2:27 1-4
Lydia Thompson, by Wild Wagoner, by G. M. Patchen........ 2:27 1-2
Draco, by Young Morrill....................................... 2:27 1-2
Rapid, by Toronto Chief, to saddle............................ 2:27 1-2
Chicago Jack, by Merrick Horse, to saddle.................... 2:27 1-2
Clarence.. 2:27 1-2
Commodore Nutt, by Grantham Chief, by Royal George....... 2:27 1-2
Mollie, Delphi's dam, by Abd-el-Kader........................ 2:27 1-2
Black Douglass, by Henry Clay................................ 2:27 1-2
Ed White... 2:27 1-2
Dreadnaught.. 2:27 1-2
Mambrino Pilot, by Mambrino Chief, dam by Pilot, to saddle... 2:27 1-2
Traveler.. 2:27 1-2
Sleepy John, dam by Red Bird................................. 2:27 1-2
Shark, by Hambletonian, dam the grandam of Dexter, to saddle.. 2:27 3-4
Shep. Knap, Jr., by Shep. Knap, he by Eaton Horse.......... 2:27 3-4
Jessie Wales, by Ajax, double................................. 2:27 3-4
Darkness, by Mambrino Chief, grandam by Pilot, double...... 2:27 3-4
James H. Burke, (late Governor Morgan)...................... 2:27 3-4
Belle of Saratoga, by Vermont Black Hawk.................... 2:28
Auburn Horse, by Champion................................... 2:28
Fannie Lee, by Ethan Allen, dam by Sherman's Black Hawk... 2:28
Black Harry Clay, by Neaves' C. M. Clay, Jr., dam by imp. Bellfounder... 2:28
Blackbird... 2:28
Dutchess... 2:28
Pelham... 2:28
Rocket... 2:28
Young Woful.. 2:28
Independence... 2:28
J. M. Botts, by Spaulding's Abdallah......................... 2:28
Jilt... 2:28

Blonde, by Hoagland's Messenger, dam by Abdallah............ 2:28
Dutchman, a second mile to saddle.... .... 2:28
Mohawk, Jr., by son of Long Island Black Hawk............... 2:28
Lady Shannon, by Harris' Hambletonian....................... 2:28
Tartar, by Royal George..................................... 2:28
Grey Jack, of Morgan blood.................................. 2:28 1-4
Miller's Damsel, by Andrew Jackson.......................... 2:28 1-4
Twang, by Iliatoga, dam by Am. Eclipse...................... 2:28 1-4
Strideaway.. 2:28 1-2
Charlie Green, by son of Abdallah........................... 2:28 1-2
Lady Garfield... 2:28 1-2
Rattler... 2:28 1-2
Jim Porter.. 2:28 1-2
Lady Shannon.. 2:28 1-2
Mary, by G. M. Patchen...................................... 2:28
B. Gen. McClellan, by Drew.................................. 2.28 1-2
Lady Vernon... 2:28 1-2
Blackstone Belle, by Brandywine, he by Abdallah............. 2:28 1-2
Young Columbus, by Columbus, dam Black Maria, grandam of
    Harris' Hambletonian.................................... 2:28 1-2
Medoc... 2:28 1-2
Lew Sayers.. 2:28 3-4
Jas. D. McMann.. 2:28 3-4
Morrissy, by Black Warrior.................................. 2:28 3-4
Fannie Kemble:.. 2:28 3-4
Lady Sheridan 2:28 3-4
Grey Hawk... 2:28 3-4
Dutchman, (formerly Derby,) by Rough and Ready.............. 2:28 3-4
Joe Hooker, Jr., by Tom Hyer, a Black Hawk.................. 2:28 3-4
Drift, (formerly Norwood,) by Hambletonian, dam by Saltram. 2:29
Lew Pettee, by Norman....................................... 2:29
Widow McCree, by American Star.... .... 2:29
Western New York, by Nonpareil, (son of Long Island Black
    Hawk,) dam by Rysdyk's Hambletonian..................... 2:29
H. B. Patchen, by G. M. Patchen............................. 2:29
Red Cloud... 2:29
Woful, by Long Island Black Hawk............................ 2:29
Medoc, Wh... 2:29
Tom Parker.. 2:29
Bally Lewis, by Pilot Jr.................................... 2:29
Miller's Damsel, by Edmond's Jackson, son of Andrew Jackson. 2:29

Reindeer, by Monmouth Eclipse	2:29
Zac Taylor, by Quimby Horse	2:29
Honest Allen, by Ethan Allen, double	2:29
Draco, by Young Morrill	2:29
Lady Sherman, by North Horse	2:29
Contraband, dam by thoroughbred	2:29
Old Man's Mare, by Young Andrew Jackson	2:29
Nelly Holcomb	2:29
Ella Elwood	2:29
N. B. Palmer	2:29
Putnam	2:29
Fleetwood	2:29
Rosamond, by Columbus	2:29
Tib Woodward	2:29
Major Edsall, by Alexander's Abdallah, dam by American Star	2:29
Up and Up	2:29
Grit	2:29
Nabocklish, by Rising Sun	2:29
Pilot, by Pilot, Jr	2:29 1-4
Ed Foster, by Young St Lawrence	2:29 1-4
Fanny Lee, by Ethan Allen, dam by the North Horse	2:29 1-4
Lexington, by Lexington	2:29 1-4
Edna	2:29 1-4
Bally Lewis, by American Star	2:29 1-2
Fearless, by Meeker Horse	2:29 1-2
Bruno, by Hambletonian	2:29 1-2
Harvest Queen, by Hambletonian, dam by American Star	2:29 1-2
New Berlin Girl	2:29 1-2
India Rubber, by Comet	2:29 1-2
Jake Oakley, by Long Island Black Hawk	2:29 1-2
Warwick, by Ethan Allen, dam Rachel	2:29 1-2
Dutch Girl, by Grey Eagle	2:29 1-2
Madawska Maid	2:29 1-2
John Fero, by imp. Consternation	2:29 1-2
Daisy Burns, by Skenado	2:29 3-4
Mountain Maid, by Morrill	2:29 3-4
Safe	2:29 3-4
Lady Ross, by Vergenes' Black Hawk, dam a Clay mare, grandam a Star mare	2:29 3-4
Lady Hughes, by Jupiter, dam by Weber's Tom Thumb	2:30
Lady Moscow	2:30

Old Put, by Clarion.. 2:30
Lady Sutton, by Morgan Eagle...................................... 2:30
Lady Augusta, by Hambletonian, dam by Saltram.............. 2:30
Lady Vernon... 2:30
Lady Jane.. 2:30
Bashaw Maid, by Plow Boy, by Long Island Black Hawk....... 2:30
Rose of Washington, by Smith Burr's Washington, saddle...... 2:30
Empress 2:30
W. H. Taylor, by Norman.. 2:30
Norman... 2:30
Young Ripton.. 2:30
Black Ralph, by Vermont Black Hawk............................ 2:30
Black Harry, double... 2:30
Emperor 2:30
India Rubber, Comet... 2:30
Centreville, by Henry Clay, dam by Mambrino.................. 2:30
Uxbridge 3:30
Copper Bottom.. 2:30
Miller's Maid.. 2:30
Tarquin... 2:30
Tom Parker 2:36
Western Metropolis... 2:30
Fanny Pullen 2:30
Long Island.. 2:30
Ike Cook, by Abdallah 2:30
Joe Hooker.. 2:30
Silas... 2:30
Whitebird, by Whitebird, a thoroughbred 2:30
Mazeppa.. 2:30
St. Elmo, by Alexander's Abdallah............................... 2:30
Jack Rossiter.. 2:30
Strathmore 2:30
Sunnyside.. 2:30
Carrol (by Cardinal), by Vermont Black Hawk................. 2:30
Champagne, by Ed Forrest 2:30
Dan Mace.. 2:30
General McClennan, by Drew..................................... 2:30
Washington Irving, by Ethan Allen, to saddle.................. 2:30
Belle of Toronto, by Royal George............................... 2:30
Denmark 2:30

Jack Stewart, by Tom Wonder, dam by Harris' Hambletonian.. 2:30
Lady Hamilton... 2:30
Purity, by Blue Bull, dam by Daniel Boone..................... 2:30
Western... 2:30

www.ingramcontent.com/pod-product-compliance
Lightning Source LLC
Chambersburg PA
CBHW030313170426
43202CB00009B/988